Nuclear
Illusion
and
Reality

Nuclear Illusion and Reality

Solly Zuckerman

Vintage Books
A Division of Random House
New York

Library of Congress Cataloging in Publication Data
Zuckerman, Solly, Lord, 1904-
Nuclear illusion and reality.
Reprint. Originally published: New York:
Viking Press, 1982.
Includes bibliographical references and index.
1. Atomic warfare. I. Title.
UF767.Z8   1983   355'.0217   82-40419
ISBN 0-394-71363-X

Manufactured in the United States of America

CONTENTS

ACKNOWLEDGEMENTS

I wish to put on record my gratitude to **Dr.**
Richard L. Garwin, IBM Fellow, and
Professor at the Center for Science and
International Affairs, Harvard University, who
allowed me to call on his vast experience in
the design and critical evaluation of modern
weaponry, including the range of nuclear
armaments, in order to check that my
simplifications of purely technical matters had
not gone too far.
I should also like to acknowledge the help
given me by Gillian Booth and Deirdre Sharp
of the Wolfson Unit in the University of East
Anglia in checking published sources and
background material.

INTRODUCTION

History books and the biographies of military leaders make it all too plain that the story of war is usually the tale of the unexpected. One side wins, the other loses, but disposing of greater force does not necessarily make for victory. Nor do the constraints that are inevitably imposed by the nature of the armaments that are available add up to a fixed set of rules. It is the unexpected that constitutes the main 'rule' of war. No one can anticipate how one or other side will react to what has not yet happened; how a military leader will plan to outwit his opponent; how his troops or the weather will behave. It is not only that. There have been times when the winner has been so exhausted by his efforts that within a few years all the fruits of victory have moved into the hands of the loser.

On the other hand, if war has no fixed rules, there are certainly conventions and laws that have been enshrined in treaty language, and which are supposed to govern its operations. One may destroy an enemy's crops, kill his citizens, but one does not poison his wells. Prisoners of war have to be treated in a humane way. Chemical warfare is outlawed by the Geneva Convention of 1925, even though some states which are party to the agreement reserve the right to use chemical weapons if they are used against them, so making their possession legitimate. The 1972 Biological and Toxin Weapons Convention bans biological warfare.

That is where the conventions of warfare end. The so-called principle of the economy of force is something different.

It is part of military doctrine, and a principle which is more a topic of discussion in staff colleges than a rule that applies to the battle field. In practice there are no agreements which limit the amount of fire-power that can be used in war, nor is there any suggestion that there should be. Today the main debate about armaments concerns the slowing down of the nuclear arms race, not the banning of the use of nuclear warheads. Some regard these merely as an extension of conventional weapons of destruction. Others hold that they are too dangerous ever to be used. And there are also those who in their pronouncements seem to believe both these propositions at the same time.

What is clear when one looks closely is that discussions of nuclear weapons fall into two distinct and logically disconnected frames of reference. The first embraces the doctrine that 'atom and hydrogen bombs' could be used to advantage in certain operations of war. The second defines the concept of deterrence. By this is meant that no sane government would embark upon military action leading to the use of nuclear weapons if this entailed the risk that it could be annihilated by a nuclear onslaught delivered by its enemy. An obvious corollary of this proposition is that in a hostile world there is no logic to a policy of unilateral disarmament for either of two countries, both of which deploy nuclear weapons. Were one to disarm, it would be placing itself at the mercy of its potential enemy. Correspondingly, it is axiomatic that the concept of mutual deterrence provides no justification for either side to increase the size of its nuclear arsenal above the minimum level that would deter.

There is, in fact, no realistic and no theoretical justification for the belief that nuclear weapons could ever be used as a rational extension of conventional armaments. As long ago as the 1961 summer meeting of NATO's military commanders I presented a summary of the results of a series of war-games which pointed to the clear conclusion that since both NATO and the USSR already possessed nuclear weapons, their use in field warfare would not only lead both sides to disaster, but also cause the deaths of hundreds of thousands, even millions, of unfortunate civilians who lived in the zone of battle. General Norstad was the Supreme Commander at the time, and the prevailing doctrine was that any Soviet intrusion into NATO territory which could not be thrown back immediately by conventional means would trigger 'massive retaliation' with nuclear weapons. 'We shall hit them with all we've got', was General Norstad's simple way of giving meaning to the phrase 'massive retaliation'. Field Marshal Montgomery also had a simple interpretation: 'I'll strike first and seek permission afterwards'.

I do not know how many of my audience followed my analysis, and its conclusion, being contrary to what was the conventional wisdom, was no doubt 'jammed' in most military minds by a barrier of accepted doctrine. But it certainly worried General Earle ('Buz') Wheeler, at the time Commander in Chief of the American forces in NATO. He asked to see me after the meeting in order to say that he had been convinced by my analysis and that, as he put it, we were 'painting ourselves into a corner' with nuclear weapons. How, he asked, were we to extricate ourselves? My answer then was what it has always been. Without an adequate conventional defence, the threat of a nuclear riposte to a non-nuclear attack was and always would be incredible. General Wheeler subsequently became the Chairman of the American Joint Chiefs of Staff, but so far as I know, his appointment did little to dissipate the false illusion of military strength that derives from the existence of NATO's nuclear armoury.

Six months after the NATO meeting, the paper which I had presented appeared in *Foreign Affairs*.[1] Harold Macmillan, then Prime Minister, was immediately challenged in the House of Commons by the opposition front bench to say that the publication of such heresy by a full-time government servant implied a change in the UK's policy with respect to nuclear weapons. His answer was: 'No Sir. They authorised the article because they thought it a valuable contribution to the discussion of these military questions.'[2]

Twenty years have now passed, and there is still no essential difference in NATO doctrine. The shibboleth of massive retaliation was replaced by Mr McNamara's 'full options' policy and then by that of 'flexible response'. But the facts remain the same — only more so. The Western powers have not forsworn 'the first use' of nuclear weapons, which implies that were NATO territory ever to be invaded by Warsaw Pact troops, and if the incursion could not be held by conventional arms, the Western command would not hesitate to resort to the use of nuclear weapons.

This continues to be NATO doctrine, even though the multiplication of the numbers and kinds of nuclear warheads in the armouries of the two sides since the end of the fifties, and the elaboration and diversification of the means of their delivery, have added nothing to the security of either the Western or the Warsaw Pact powers. Church leaders and statesmen, presidents and prime ministers, the leaders of the Soviet Communist Party, as well as military leaders on both sides, have declared that, however it were to begin, a nuclear war could not be contained, and that the result would be an incalculable disaster for mankind. On both sides those who should know now warn that neither the Warsaw Pact nor the NATO alliance could win a nuclear war. Even the present Chairman of the NATO Military Committee, Admiral Robert Falls, has added his warning that the Western alliance is imperilled by its reliance on nuclear weapons.[3] Clearly the many who proclaim the contrary message are only serving as the vehicle for blind military propaganda.

In a pessimistic statement about the fear with which he viewed the nuclear arms race, General Omar Bradley, the leader of the American armies in Europe in World War II,

and later also chairman of the Joint Chiefs of Staff, remarked
as far back as 1957 that what worried him most was not 'the
magnitude of the problem, but ... our colossal indifference
to it'.[4] President Eisenhower, Supreme Commander of the
Allied Forces in World War II, was equally explicit. Others
have expressed similar sentiments. In the House of Commons
Defence Debate of 28 April, 1980, Sir John Eden, a Conserv-
ative spokesman, said; 'It is vital that the people are alerted to
the real risks.'[5]

I have therefore written this short book in the hope that what
Harold Macmillan said in 1962 is still valid; that nothing but
good can come from the ventilation of the facts. My own
view is that only if there is a widespread understanding of the
realities of possible destruction might there be an answer,
before it is too late, to the question: How can the world be
extricated from the nuclear corner into which it has been
painted?

I have been deeply involved for more than thirty years,
many of them officially, in the matters that are discussed in
this book, in the writing of which there has been no need to
call on classified official documents. The whole story is in the
public domain, particularly in the United States. I have also
drawn on several articles which I published after the one that
appeared in *Foreign Affairs*; in particular on a few sections
from my *Scientists and War*[6] which appeared in 1966, and
which is now out of print; and on an address that I gave to
the American Philosophical Society in November 1979, under
the title *Science Advisers and Scientific Advisers*, and which was
published as a pamphlet by the Menard Press in London in
1980. I need to make it clear that the opinions and views
which I express here are my own. They cannot be taken as
representing the present UK Government's views, any more
than what I published in 1962 did those of the then
Government.

Unfortunately, the 'colossal indifference' to what continues to be one of mankind's most urgent problems cannot be corrected without some reference to technicalities. I have limited these to the minimum possible, even at the risk of offending specialists by my simplifications, and have tried to confine most to my first chapter — which can be skimmed by those who are put off by such matters. For the same reason I have attempted to focus where possible, and so far as words allow, on the facts of destruction, not on numbers of warheads and delivery vehicles. I have done so because the general reader who is concerned with these matters must surely have become mesmerised by the outpourings of amateur strategists who disguise their lack of direct experience of destruction and social breakdown behind a smokescreen of numbers. For those who prefer these things, there are enough books which provide enumerations of warheads and delivery systems.

The central facts are merely lost in technicalities. What matters is that a nuclear exchange could blot out civilization in both the Eurasiatic and North American continents; that nuclear warheads are too dangerous to use in war; and that while nuclear weapon states might be deterred from turning their nuclear arsenals on each other, the existence of nuclear weapons can neither prevent war nor defend in war.

Nuclear Illusion and Reality

CHAPTER I

The Nuclear Arsenal

Before the era of nuclear weapons, the biggest single piece of destruction that could be caused by any one weapon in the normal operations of war was set by the maximum weight of bomb that could be carried in an aircraft. It was trivial in the light of what can be done today. The heaviest bombs that were produced in the Second World War did not exceed ten tons in weight, and were devised for special tasks such as breaching reinforced concrete defences three or more metres thick (for example, the roofs of submarine pens). The so-called 'block-busters' that were used in attacks on cities weighed four tons, while the vast majority of the bombs that were dropped varied in weight between 50 kg and 1000 kg, the radius of the area of destruction caused by the blast increasing, theoretically, in proportion to the cube root of the weight of the explosive it contained. However much damage cities suffered, the total area that conventional bombs could destroy was the sum of a varying number of pockmarks of damage. Thus sixteen square miles of Tokyo were burnt out in March 1945 by tens and tens of thousands of small incendiary bombs that rained down over more than one hundred square miles[7].

The vital difference between conventional and nuclear weapons is that while for all practical purposes there is a limit to the amount of destruction that can be caused by the explosion of a conventional bomb, there is none for a nuclear warhead. Hiroshima and then Nagasaki were each wiped out by a single atomic bomb. Together they weighed about the same as the 10-ton 'Grandslam' that had been designed for the Royal Air Force for use in special attacks against the most heavily built viaducts. The explosive power — 'yield' in the jargon — of those two primitive nuclear weapons was registered in units equivalent to the blast of 1000 tons of conventional explosive — a kiloton, or kt, of yield. Plus or minus one or two kt, they were rated at about 15 kt; that is to say, the equivalent of fifteen thousand tons of conventional explosive.

The first two atomic bombs owed their destructive power to the instantaneous release of a fabulous amount of energy as the atoms of the explosive material of the two bombs 'split'. The process of atomic splitting is called fission. The explosive material in both cases was man-made, one being an unstable very heavy metal consisting of the atoms of Uranium 235, and the other its close relative Plutonium. Small fission bombs are today the trigger mechanism of hydrogen ('fusion') bombs, whose much greater destructive power is due to the release of energy that accompanies, not the splitting or fission of very heavy atoms such as those of Uranium, but the fusion of variants, known as isotopes, of the atoms of the lightest element — hydrogen — that exists in the chemical scale.

Today, ten times, a hundred times, the amount of explosive power that wiped out Hiroshima and Nagasaki can be packed in a single warhead weighing less than a fifth of either of the first two nuclear devices.

The explosive power of hydrogen bombs is usually measured in terms of megatons. A megaton is a thousand kilotons, and today a megaton warhead is just an ordinary-sized weapon in the nuclear armouries of the USA and USSR and, to a lesser extent, of those of the UK, France and China; one million tons of conventional explosive in, let us say, a 500-lb package — the exact weight is immaterial. The most powerful warhead that has ever been tested had a yield estimated at 58 megatons. It was exploded in the final series of atmospheric nuclear tests that the Soviet Union carried out in 1962. Khrushchev, then the Soviet leader, declared that the bomb might have been made bigger, but then all the windows in Moscow, some four thousand miles from the testing ground, might have been shattered by the blast.

The two 'bombs' that devastated Hiroshima and Nagasaki were the only two nuclear explosive devices then in existence. There has been endless discussion about the strategic and moral justification for the decision to use them. Some argue that the destruction of the two cities was necessary to end Japanese resistance. Others who have studied the evidence hold that Japan was already finished. But whatever the rights or wrongs of the decision, the demonstration of the destructive power of the weapons not surprisingly initiated a nuclear arms race. The Soviet Union exploded her first test bomb in 1949, Britain in 1952. In 1960 came France, and China in 1964. India exploded a nuclear device in 1974.

Since most, or perhaps all, technological developments derive from common basic scientific knowledge, all real secrecy vanished with the demonstration that an atomic explosion was possible. In any event, there never was any 'secret' about the atom bomb, either for the Russians or for the British, or indeed even for other countries, especially after the American Government decided to publish, in 1945, the famous Smyth Report on Atomic Energy[8]. Obviously there will always be refinements of one sort or another in the making of warheads that must be kept secret, and obviously, too, only countries which can command the necessary technical and industrial expertise and facilities can make bombs. But there is no reason to suppose that the five countries which already manufacture nuclear weapons will necessarily close the list of nuclear-weapons powers.

After all, an American student recently achieved fame by providing a description of the way a hydrogen bomb is made — together with diagrams that gave what were assumed to be the correct dimensions. He described the primary trigger fission device, as well as the secondary explosive material which is the source of the isotopes of the hydrogen atom (deuterium and tritium), whose fusion leads to so fabulous a release of energy.

The two atomic bombs that were dropped on Japan in 1945 were as crude in relation to modern nuclear weapons as a terrorist's home-made grenade would be to a modern armour-piercing shell. No one knows the exact number of nuclear warheads that exist in the world today, but according to a recent and authoritative United Nations report[9], it is probably 'in excess of 40,000', with their explosive power ranging 'from about 100 tons up to more than 20 million tons equivalent of chemical high explosive.' The Report goes on to say, 'The largest weapon ever tested released an energy approximately four thousand times that of the atomic bomb that levelled Hiroshima, and there is in principle no upper limit to the explosive yield that may be attained. The total strength of present nuclear arsenals may be equivalent to about one million Hiroshima bombs, i.e. some thirteen thousand million tons of TNT. It is often pointed out that this is equivalent to more than 3 tons for every man, woman and child on the earth.' The armoury of nuclear weapons now includes free-falling bombs, warheads for ballistic missiles, artillery shells, depth charges, nuclear-tipped torpedoes, with yields ranging from a kiloton to several megatons. 'Small' weapons have also been devised for use in field warfare.

The warheads that have been made by the nuclear powers are only a proportion of those that designers have tried out over the years. For example, there was once a proposal to issue a 'sub-kiloton' nuclear weapon called the Davy Crockett, which was so light that it could be carried by individual infantrymen. Since it was obvious from the start that the dispersed deployment of such weapons would make it impossible to control their use, the Davy Crockett, although in production, was soon withdrawn from service. The so-called neutron bomb, which has been so much in the news in recent years, was first discussed in the fifties and has always been technically feasible. Two different kinds of energetic and electrically uncharged sub-nuclear particles, gamma rays and neutrons, are released when the nucleus of an atom splits (i.e. undergoes fission), or when the nuclei of the heavy isotopes of hydrogen fuse. All these particles are dangerous. X-rays are one variety of neutral particle and, as is well-known, they can penetrate for varying distances into materials, including the body. The different kinds of sub-atomic particles that are released into the atmosphere after a nuclear explosion also travel finite but different distances. In effect, the neutron bomb would be a small hydrogen bomb, the idea being that its main lethal effects would be exercised, not by the blast of the explosion, but by the radiation of neutrons which, while electrically neutral, transmit great energy.

Now the area of destruction caused by the blast from the usual kind of nuclear warhead far exceeds that due to nuclear radiation. As the recent United Nations Report[9] on nuclear weapons both indicates and implies, for warheads of inter-mediate and large yields — that is to say, with explosive yields in excess of a few kt — the radius of the area of destruction due to blast is doubled when the yield is increased eight times. If the area that would be devastated by the blast of a bomb with a yield of 10 kt extends, say, to 1 km (0.62 of a mile) from the explosion, it would take a bomb of 80 kt, that is to say, one with eight times the yield, to reach out to twice that distance. On the other hand, for yields of fusion weapons in the range of 0.5 kt to 4 kt, such an increase would add only about 250 metres to the radius of the area in which the intensity of radiation (which could, of course, pass through walls or through the armour of a tank) would immediately prove lethal. 'A hypothetical "neutron bomb" which derived *all* its energy from fusion would at 10-kiloton yield have about equal radius of blast kill and radiation kill.' But 'for a hypothetical 1-kt ER (enhanced radiation) weapon, the zone of danger due to neutrons would considerably exceed that due to blast'. Thus, the 'enhanced radiation bomb' as represented by the neutron bomb, should more properly be called a 'suppressed blast weapon'. The neutron bomb would be more costly to manufacture and has more constraints in its delivery than does a 10-kt weapon of the *same* 'radiation kill-range and greater blast kill'[9].

It should be noted here that the pressure of the blast or shock wave generated both by conventional and nuclear explosives falls off as the wave moves from the point of burst. Let us say that up to a pressure of x lbs per square inch, above that of the 15 lbs per square inch of atmospheric pressure, all solidly-built structures would be destroyed, and that the critical distance at which the pressure falls below the x level is y km from the burst. Then — to re-emphasise a point that I have already made — if it were to take a warhead with a yield of, say, 125 kt to generate a blast wave with this pressure at y km, it would take one with a yield eight times as much, i.e. a megaton, to have the same effect at 2y km. In contrast, 'the area of destruction due to blast increases in proportion to the number of weapons. This means in practice that the destruction is increased by increasing the number of warheads and lowering their individual yield, i.e. one large warhead is not so effective as several smaller ones of the same total yield spread out over the target area.'[9] The same is true of chemical bombs, given that they are sufficient to deal with the targets for which they are designed. Thus, analysis of the killing power of the bombs dropped on London in the Second World War showed that total bomb-load for bomb-load, 50 kg bombs were much more effective than were the bigger bombs that were used[10].

As more and more nuclear warheads have been designed and produced, major developments have also occurred in what are called 'delivery systems'. Except in so far as they denote increasing accuracy of fire, there is nothing basically novel about the developments of the past two decades that have been made in aircraft, in field guns, in depth charges, or in torpedoes. Aiming techniques for free-falling bombs were simple in the first years of the Second World War, and improved enormously towards its end. They have gone on improving. Radar targeting is now commonplace in air, land and sea warfare. The development of computers, of pre-set programmed instructions, of servo-mechanisms which automatically alter the aiming of a gun, have brought about miracles in the elaboration of armaments. An airman today could identify more than a single hostile opponent on his airborne radar, 'lock on' his navigational and aiming devices, and follow particular 'blips' until the enemy aircraft were within firing range, when his rockets would be automatically released. Anti-aircraft and ship-to-ship fire are also automatically controlled, whether by advanced techniques in the fields of radar, sonar, or heat (i.e. infra-red technology). And, of course, we now have orbiting space satellites to help report what 'lies on the other side of the hill', whether by film which can differentiate between objects a few feet apart, or by digitalised radio pulses from which a picture can be built up either in terms of visual or 'heat-profiles'.

But for all these technical miracles, the technology that has most transformed, and produced the greatest confusion in the nuclear world is that of the ballistic missile. In the

Second World War there was the V1, a small pilotless aircraft which carried a charge of 850 kg of high explosive, and the V2, the prototype of the ballistic rocket of today. The V1, a very inaccurate even if spectacular weapon, was launched from a ramp after being pointed in the direction of its intended target, on to which it descended when its motors cut out. The V2 descended through the atmosphere like a bolt from the blue, and since it gave no warning of its impending descent, it was far more demoralising, and caused twice as many casualties, even though it carried 100 kg less explosive. It, too, was anything but accurate. But today an inter-continental ballistic rocket can make a relatively accurate hit on a target thousands of miles from its launching point.

Rockets made of up to four stages can now sweep across continents or reach to the moon and further planets. The terminal stage can house three or four men plus supplies, and lock on to space stations that orbit the globe year after year. Modern guidance systems, of which inertial gyro-platforms and mini-computers are essential parts, have given ballistic missiles an accuracy that makes it possible to land a man on a given spot on the moon, and in theory to get nuclear warheads to strike within tens of yards of their targets from five thousand or more miles away. By a process which goes by the acronym MIRV — multiple independently targetable re-entry vehicle — a single ballistic missile can carry ten or more nuclear warheads to strike that number of different aiming points. Given that the map coordinates of the launching point and intended target are precisely known — and since the days of mapping from space satellites these can be better defined now than ever before — anything seems possible, *provided that the whole system works to perfection.* Thus, a MIRVed missile would be launched on to a calculated ballistic path outside the atmosphere. The times when it will reach specific points on its ballistic path are known. If the missile is carrying several warheads on a stage that is called a 'manoeuvrable bus', the speed and orientation of the bus will be altered by the automatic operation of small jet motors so that each terminal independent warhead will be separately directed on to the flight path that will take it through the atmosphere and on to its pre-set target. It is claimed that re-entry vehicles could also be fitted with their own sensor systems to allow them to make the necessary corrections, when on their terminal paths, by the automatic comparison of the signals received with pre-set computer maps they carry of the target.

Even more elaborate navigational and guidance techniques have been designed for the low-flying subsonic cruise missile, which in effect is a development of the V1 of the Second World War. The vehicle carries radar and computer systems by which its course is steered in relation to an altitude map with which its memory store is furnished; that is to say, a map showing altitude features for selected segments of its flight-path to a pre-set target. Forward- and sideways-looking radar equipment of a similar kind is fitted into low-flying aircraft to permit of what is called 'automatic contour flying'. Other sensors, too, can be used to act as the stimulus in the servo-mechanisms of navigational and arming systems. Skybolt, an air-launched ballistic missile on which $500 million was spent before it was cancelled, was fitted with a star-tracking navigational system. In theory, ballistic missiles launched from submarines are not as accurate as their land-based equivalents, even though they have the same guidance system, the reason being that the coordinates of the launch point at sea cannot be as accurately determined. However, computers and accurate sonar applied to the launcher (or navigation-satellite receiver computers on the submarine-launched missiles themselves) can now accord to such missiles accuracies thus far achievable only from those launched from land.

When a ballistic missile is said to be accurate to so many yards or metres, what is meant is that both calculation and such tests as have been made indicate that fifty percent of shots fired at a given target will fall within a circle of that particular radius whose centre is the aiming point (the jargon term is that the missile has a CEP — 'circular error probable' — of so many yards or metres). But such estimates of accuracy presuppose that every step in the process from launch to strike works according to plan: the start of the ballistic path, the rate of burn of the fuel, the operation of the navigational jets, the angle of re-entry, the 'resistance' of the atmosphere, and so on. Furthermore, both the Americans and Russians test their ballistic missiles on East/West or West/East trajectories, whereas were they ever used in anger they would be directed over the North Pole. They would then be subjected to different gravitational conditions, different densities of the upper atmosphere, and unknown wind velocities. But above all, what the calculation of CEPs does not mean is that the fifty percent of the shots which it is estimated will fall *outside* a given radius will necessarily have a 'normal distribution', that is to say, will tail off from the aiming point in a regular and ascertainable way. In other words, a ballistic missile with a declared CEP of, say, 400 yards, might, when fired, fail to operate according to plan, and strike a mile or five miles from its intended target. The laws of statistics are like that.

CHAPTER 2

Nuclear Destruction

The destruction of Hiroshima and Nagasaki in August 1945 ended World War II. 70,000 people were killed in a flash in Hiroshima, 40,000 in Nagasaki.[11] Another 100,000 had died by the end of 1945. Deaths due to the chronic effects of radiation have gone on being registered ever since.

The figures of casualties are to some extent estimates, but they give a true picture of what a 'small' nuclear bomb can do. The fact that Nagasaki did not suffer as many casualties as Hiroshima was due to its different layout. Hiroshima is spread out on a plain, Nagasaki is built in a series of valleys.

A one-megaton hydrogen bomb detonated over a modern European or American city with a population of, say, a million plus, would lead to the immediate death of about a third of the population. This conclusion is derived from analyses based upon the measured effects of test nuclear explosions. Blast and fire are the two factors which do most of the immediate damage. As I have said (p. 20), the blast (ie shock wave) of a nuclear warhead has the same general characteristics as that produced by the explosion of TNT, but because of the far greater energy released by a nuclear explosion, a vastly greater area is devastated. What happens is that the 'matter' that is embodied as solid in a small mass is, as it were, instantaneously converted into a balloon of, let us call it, gas. The balloon expands at supersonic speed, the speed falling off as its front, which is the shock wave, moves from the point of explosion. So does the pressure in the front. This is enormous at the start. In the case of a one-megaton explosion, it is still 5 lbs above atmospheric pressure at some four miles from the centre of the explosion. At that distance the wind behind the front is moving at a speed of nearly 200 miles an hour. That is the speed of the worst hurricanes ever recorded; for example, the one that devastated the town of Darwin in Australia in 1974 reached a speed of only 175 miles an hour. Even setting aside for a moment instantaneous flash burns, fires, radiation and radioactive fallout, that gives some idea of what the term nuclear explosion means.

Blast accounts for about half the energy that the nuclear explosion generates. A single one-megaton bomb would demolish solidly-built houses up to two miles from the point of burst. Although thermal effects account for only about a third of the energy that is released, the fires that would be caused, given the right conditions, could cover an area far greater than that damaged by blast. The rest of the energy of the bomb takes the form of nuclear radiation.

For practical purposes, the characteristics of explosions of a given yield can be regarded as constant. We know how the pressure of the shock or blast wave falls off as it moves from the centre of the burst at a speed far greater than that of sound. We know the size of the area which would suffer from radioactive contamination and with what declining intensity; we know the area which would be at risk from instantaneous fires.

Analyses of the nature of the destruction caused with ordinary bombs during the Second World War indicate, however, that when considering the effects of nuclear weapons, it would be instructive to take into account not just the physical effects of the explosion, but the particular characteristics of the targets that might be hit. That is what was done in the first detailed analysis that was made of the likely effects of a megaton explosion on a city, the English city of Birmingham being chosen as the hypothetical target. The reason for the detail of that analysis, which was made in 1960 and the results of which were spelt out in the 1968 UN *Report on the Effects of Nuclear Weapons*,[12] is that cities and towns vary in their layout and in the density and distribution of their populations; the density of housing varies in different part of the city; the water supply of one town comes in and is distributed differently from that of another; power stations are not sited in a uniform fashion; sewerage systems differ in their layout; food markets are variously distributed, as are also hospitals. In short, there is no uniform pattern to a city, nor do we find that within a city one district exactly reproduces another. It should also be remembered that if a city were attacked by a nuclear weapon or weapons, the results would vary according to the position of the burst or bursts, both in relation to the geography of the city and to the time of the attack.

Because of these variations, the way to achieve a realistic picture of the effects of a nuclear burst over a populated area is to focus on a city or town, the details of whose layout can be taken into account, and to build up the story from the sum of the likely events as they would affect the smallest urban units that are defined for normal administrative purposes. Only in that way can one start to derive a 'human picture' of what would happen.

Birmingham is the centre of a conurbation, its built-up area running into those of several small towns. At the time of the 1960 analysis, the population of the city's administrative area was estimated to be about a million. It was assumed that the city had been struck by a single megaton bomb exploded close to ground level about a mile from its centre.

The city would have been totally destroyed up to a distance of about two miles from the point of burst of the bomb. Within this area there would have been practically no survivors. Fires would have been raging and spreading. Barely a house in the whole of the greater Birmingham area would not have been damaged to a greater or lesser extent. The analysis showed that only about a third would still have been habitable, and that roofs, doors, and windows would have been damaged everywhere. Depending on the direction of the prevailing wind, the whole built-up area of the conurbation to one or other side of the point of burst would have been affected by radioactive fallout.

Essential services would have ceased to exist in the main area of destruction. What remained elsewhere depended entirely upon the way the services had been laid out. Parts of the city which had only been slightly affected by the direct effects of the blast, or even by radioactive fallout, were without water or drainage, power supplies or food supplies. Hospitals had been destroyed.

Detailed analysis showed that a third of the city's inhabitants would have been killed immediately as a result of blast and fire, or would have died from a lethal dose of radiation in the first two days. Most of the dead would have been killed by the blast wave, which would have torn houses apart, and in the debris of which survivors would have remained trapped. There would have been a hundred thousand serious casualties who would have been unable to look after themselves, as well as tens of thousand not so severely wounded. This means that only about half of Birmingham's original population would have been alive and in a condition to try to cope with the situation by which they would have been immediately confronted.

Numbers of them would later have become casualties from radiation. Those who had been trapped in the wreckage of buildings and who could still fend for themselves would have known that if they themselves could not crawl to safety, the chances would be that there would be no one to help them. Able survivors would be either fleeing or searching for food, for relatives, for help, or for some place of shelter better than the one in which they happened to be when the bomb went off.

In short, the explosion of a single megaton weapon over one of the largest cities in the United Kingdom would almost inevitably lead to its total elimination.

If one could concentrate into one focal point and one focal moment all the destruction which Britain suffered in the Second World War, the picture would not be as bad as the one that needs to be conjured up when one talks of the explosion of a single megaton weapon over a city. However improbable it may be that such a thing could ever happen, one also has to remember that were it to do so, it would not be just one city which would have been attacked, but several, and not one megaton on a target, but several.

If Birmingham were ever a target, the chances are that Coventry, Bristol, Manchester, Liverpool, not to speak of London, would also have been targets. We have to compound the picture of disaster I have painted. There would be no central services, no communications, no quarter to which survivors could turn. It is easy to say that if a third of the population of a city of a million were killed instantly, two-thirds would still be alive. But what would they be able to do? Two in three doctors would probably not be alive, nor two in three hospitals standing. Nor would there be two in three firemen with their stations intact. Nor two in three sewerage and water workers. Nor two in three railwaymen or telephone operators. That kind of subtraction is fantasy. Since there are few cities in the UK with a population of more than a million, we also have to remember that a megaton burst over a smaller city with a population of, say, a quarter of a million, would be an even greater disaster, if that is possible to imagine.

The general picture revealed by this analysis of 1960 has been confirmed these past few years in reports of official studies that have recently been made in the United States in order to provide Congress with a picture of what would happen if an American city were struck by a one-megaton weapon. One such study, which focused on Detroit, was carried out by the Office of Technology Assessment and published in 1979.[13]

The built-over area of Detroit was estimated to have a population of some 4.3 million inhabitants, and it was assumed that it had been attacked at night without warning. It was also assumed that no other city had been attacked, and that outside help would therefore be available.

The analysis showed that a single megaton warhead burst at surface level would kill a quarter of a million people straight away, and that half a million would be wounded, presenting 'a medical task of incredible magnitude ... the total medical facilities of the United States will be severely overburdened'. Seventy square miles of property would be destroyed, while fire would cause even more damage. There would be an 'immediate loss of power in a major sector of the total US power grid'. If the one-megaton bomb were to burst at 6,000 feet, the number of fatalities would be almost doubled, and that of the injured greatly increased. If instead of a one-megaton bomb a 25-megaton bomb were to be responsible for the disaster, three-quarters of the population would be either killed or wounded instantly.

As a rule of thumb, the American experts on nuclear weapons regard the lethal area of a warhead as being defined by the radius of a circle within which it is estimated that the number of survivors would equal the number of fatalities outside, with the obvious proviso that population density is roughly the same over the whole area. The Americans also take it as a rule of thumb that no ordinary building can stand up to an excess pressure of 5 lbs, and that the lethal area of a bomb for fatal casualties can be regarded as

Dear 8th CD:

If you are interested in havi
with Freeze activists from other D.
next in Massachusetts in our Freez

POTLUCK SUPPER, Saturday, Nov

Beth Wray's home, 16 Emerson

<u>RSVP</u>: to Beth Wray at 232-1

It's OK to bring spouses f

extending to the 5 lb limit, beyond which both the velocity and pressure of the shock wave rapidly fall off.

In a general article published in *Scientific American* in July 1979,[14] Kevin N. Lewis has noted that the human body is much more resistant to the direct impact of a blast or shock wave than is, say, the wall of a building. This fact was established during the Second World War on the basis of extrapolations from the results of experimental studies, as well as from an analysis of air-raid casualties.[10] Unfortunately the resistance of the human frame to the violent shock imparted by a long-duration supersonic wave-front travelling at pressures well above atmospheric pressure is a purely academic matter in the context of a nuclear explosion. However resistant to the direct effects of blast, a person within the lethal zone of an explosion could not escape dying a thousand deaths — from violent displacement, from being hit by flying debris, from being buried under rubble with no hope of rescue.

In his article, Kevin Lewis uses the accepted criteria to describe what would happen to the Boston area of Massachusetts if it were attacked with ten one-megaton warheads. He writes that an over-pressure down to 5 lbs per square inch would affect an area of more that 500 square miles. He goes on to say:

'More than 1.3 million people would be killed by the prompt blast and thermal effects of the explosions, and more than 80 per cent of the area's industrial capacity would be destroyed. It is likely that the secondary effects of the explosions, particularly fires and fallout, would increase these totals.

'If conditions were favorable to the attack, the most devastating effect might be incendiary. Under certain weather conditions each one-megaton burst could ignite fires as much as 10 miles away. In such an attack a fire threat would presumably exist throughout much of eastern

Massachusetts. Flash-induced fires would be joined by blast-triggered fires from toppled furnaces, stoves and boilers. Scattered debris and ruptured tanks and pipelines would add fuel to the fires. Firebreaks would be bridged by materials hurled by the blast. After the attack the suppression of possibly hundreds of small fires per acre would be a monumental task; water mains would be shattered and firefighting equipment and crews would be destroyed or disabled.

'Depending on weather conditions and the characteristics of the target area (particularly the density of flammable structures), the many individual fires might consolidate into one of two types of mass fire: a firestorm or a conflagration. A firestorm is driven by a strong vertical updraft of heated air, which is replaced by cool air sucked in from the periphery of the fire. A conflagration is driven in addition by a strong ground wind that was present before the attack. Whereas a firestorm continues only as long as its centripetal winds do, a conflagration can continue as long as fuel is available.

'The consequence of a mass fire is total devastation within the affected area.'

Were a single megaton warhead to explode over a city such as New York, say over the centre of Manhattan, the blast would rip through skyscrapers, turning vast panels and chunks of concrete and steel into high-velocity secondary missiles that would smash their way for hundreds of yards. The picture is all but unimaginable. Hiroshima, built mainly of one-storey houses with a few multi-storey structures, was laid waste by one small bomb. A single megaton weapon would cause a far greater mess of New York. Given that the attack occurred during office hours, the explosion could kill millions. If one were to assume that no other cities were hit at the same time, and that steps could be taken to clear the area, it would take years to move the smashed concrete, the bricks, the girders — and the bodies.

The same group that provided an assessment of what would happen to Detroit were it attacked did an analysis[13] of Leningrad, which also has a metropolitan population of about 4.3 million. The estimated casualty figure as a result of the burst in the air of a one-megaton warhead was 890,000 killed, with one and a quarter million wounded. The corresponding figures for a 9-megaton warhead were 2.5 and 1.1 million. If instead of single megaton warheads the city were hit by ten 40-kt bombs (the destructive load of a single Poseidon submarine-launched missile), there would be roughly one million dead and one million wounded.

No doubt the Russians have made similar analyses of what would happen to their cities if they were to suffer a nuclear attack, and no doubt, too, they have made their own estimates of what would happen to the enemy cities which, given the outbreak of nuclear war, they might attack. The results have not been published, but at a recent meeting of medical men convened in the United States, Dr Chazov, Director General of the National Cardiology Research Centre in Moscow, is reported to have said[15] that Soviet studies have shown that were a Russian city to be hit by a one-megaton warhead, 300,000 people would be immediately killed, and another 300,000 wounded and burnt.

Not surprisingly, the broad conclusions of these analyses apply as much to small as to large towns. For example, in the early sixties a study[12] was made of the likely result were a small English town such as Carlisle to be hit by one 20-kiloton bomb. Carlisle, which then had a population of 70,000 people living in 23,000 houses, was chosen because it is an important rail centre similar to many on the Continent that would be threatened by nuclear weapons given that a nuclear 'theatre war', as it is now called, were ever to erupt. Roughly speaking, the scale of destruction turned out to be relatively the same as for the megaton weapon that had burst over a city with a population of a million. Thousands of houses would have been immediately destroyed, and others would be on fire. Not one would have escaped damage. The proportion of people killed or wounded would be the same, or a little less, than what one would expect on a *pro rata* basis with the megaton burst over a one-million city, but the survivors would have just as terrifying a problem to contend with as would those in any larger city — fires, roads blocked, no water supply, no food, radioactive fallout, and so on.

In the industrialised world in which we live, no large town is, of course, an entity in itself. It depends for its livelihood on other towns, which in turn it feeds with its products. And with the whole of the United Kingdom virtually urbanized, every centre of population is fed not only from the country's own farms, but from those of other countries as well. There is no secret about the manufacturing plants that are to be found in Sheffield or Derby or Manchester, and the sources from which these great cities receive their raw materials and food are known. There would be no difficulty in discovering what components they manufacture; to which plants in other cities these are sent; for what finished goods they are responsible. Using what information was available in the early 1960s, an analysis was once made of the 'knock-on' effects of the elimination of Leningrad alone. It turned out that much more was involved than just the destruction of the 'target'. Every great city is a critical factor in the well-being of other towns in the complex of which it is a part. No city is self-sufficient.

The analyses to which I have so far referred provide a picture of what may be called single units of nuclear destruction. It is, of course, just conceivable that were war ever to break out, and were either of the engaged sides to resort to nuclear weapons, one shot would be enough to end hostilities, without the side that was struck ever retaliating. However conceivable such an outcome, it is in the highest degree unlikely. The more probable reaction would be retaliation in kind. Only utter desperation and fear could lead one side in a conflict to a 'rational' decision to use a nuclear weapon, and if one warhead, why not more than one? The side that had not initiated the exchange would in all reason reckon that it had to respond in order to deny its enemy any advantage. If, again, one side were to launch one or more nuclear weapons by what is called 'accident', or 'inadvertence', and not as an action underwritten by the authority of its political leaders, the upshot would be the same because, 'hot line' or no 'hot line', the side that had been struck would be bound to assume that the action had been deliberate.

Were any nuclear exchange to start in which the United Kingdom was engaged, it would therefore be realistic to assume that the targets, for purpose of illustration, would be the ten largest cities in the United Kingdom. These would be: Bradford, Bristol, Birmingham, Edinburgh, Glasgow, Leeds, Liverpool, London, Manchester and Sheffield. Together they account for 22.5 per cent of the UK's total population. And if large cities were to be simultaneously struck, let us assume that each suffered two strikes with one-megaton weapons. The result would be an immediate death-roll of about ten million, with another ten million wounded, and with all the major hospitals of the country destroyed. All, or the vast majority of the UK's administrative buildings would have disappeared, rail and road communications would be totally disrupted, there would be no food supplies, industries would be without supplies, and there would be no major telephone exchanges.

I doubt if the United Kingdom would, or could *ever* recover physically from such a blow. It would not matter that towns like Aberdeen, Newcastle or Nottingham would not have been struck. They would become ghost towns, full of fear, to which survivors from the periphery of the bombed cities would flee for help. There would be radio-active fallout. Central government would, without question, be powerless, if indeed it still existed.

Several major studies have been published in the United States in recent years, describing what could be called the global effects of nuclear war. One[13], to which I have already referred in describing the effects of an attack limited to Detroit on the one hand, and Leningrad on the other, and which was carried out for the Senate Committee on Foreign Relations, also examined 'a full range of possible nuclear attacks, with attacking forces ranging in extent from a single weapon to the bulk of a superpower's arsenal.' It dealt 'explicitly with both Soviet attacks on the United States and US attacks on the Soviet Union', and was concerned with 'the multiple effects of nuclear war, indirect as well as direct, long term as well as short term, and social and economic as well as physical.'

This is what is said about the probable results of an attack against the other side's oil refineries, limited to ten 'strategic nuclear delivery vehicles only' (SNDVs, as they are called in the vernacular of SALT, ie the Strategic Arms Limitation Talks) — meaning either ballistic missiles or long-range aircraft.

'The calculations showed that the Soviet attack would destroy 64 per cent of US oil refining capacity, while the US attack would destroy 73 per cent of Soviet refining capacity. Calculations were also made of "prompt fatalities", including those killed by blast and fallout, assuming no special civil defense measures; they showed about 5 million US deaths and about 1 million Soviet deaths.

'One can only speculate about the consequences of such extensive destruction. There would have to be drastic changes in both the US and Soviet economies to cope with the sudden disappearance of the bulk of oil refining capacity. Productivity in virtually every industrial sector would decline, and some sectors would be largely wiped out.'

In a further analysis, the team considered attacks on Inter-Continental Ballistic Missile (ICBM) silos, bomber bases, and missile submarine bases. The conclusion was that 'if the attack involves surface bursts of many very large weapons, if weather conditions are unfavorable, and if no fallout shelters are created beyond those that presently exist, US deaths could reach 20 million and Soviet deaths more than 10 million.'

Finally, the Report dealt with the consequences of 'a very large attack against a range of military and economic targets', the assumption having been made that the USSR would strike first and the USA then retaliate. The deaths resulting from such an exchange 'would be far beyond any precedent. Executive branch calculations show a range of US deaths from 35 to 77 per cent (ie from 70 million to 160 million dead) and Soviet deaths from 20 to 40 per cent of the population.' The authors of the Report point out that 'the difference in damage to civilian populations and economies between a "first strike" and a "second strike" seems to lie within the range of uncertainty created by other factors.'

This, however, is not the full story. If ballistic missiles were fired at cities as well as at military and 'economic' targets, 'somewhere between 20 million and 30 million *additional* people on each side' could be killed. 'These calculations reflect only deaths during the first 30 days. Additional millions would be injured, and many would eventually die from lack of adequate medical care. In addition, millions of people might starve or freeze during the following winter, but it is not possible to estimate how many'. There would, of course, be millions more who would die slowly from the latent effects of radiation.

A second report[16], prepared for another US Congressional Committee, and also published in 1979, has the title 'Economic and Social Consequences of Nuclear Attacks on the United States'. It records the results of yet another dispassionate computer study of what would happen if the major, ie 71 'largest Standard Metropolitan Statistical Areas' of the United States were attacked with nuclear weapons. 'Approximately 123 million or 62 per cent of the American population and $177 billion or 68 per cent of US manufacturing capacity lie within the metropolitan areas (SMSAs) assumed to be the targets in the four hypothetical attacks.'

The heaviest set of attacks assumed that 500 one-megaton weapons would be directed at these targets, together with from 200 to 300 100-kiloton warheads. The lightest set of attacks assumed that apart from the kiloton strikes there would be only 100 one-megaton hits. The calculations showed that in the heaviest attacks between 35 and 45 per cent of the US population would be casualties; in the lightest between 20 and 30 per cent. 'The smallest attack would cause about 20 to 30 per cent casualties among the US population, and would destroy 25 to 35 per cent of total manufacturing capacity and 45 to 55 per cent of the manufacturing capacity in the 71 largest metropolitan areas. When the number of one-megaton weapons in the attack is increased five-fold (500 per cent) casualties and industrial damage only increase by approximately two fold.'

In the language of the Report, 'significant economic disruption and social disorganization could be achieved even with the smaller attacks since they also produce substantial loss of life and property and significant secondary effects. Presumably, smaller attacks would be designed to strike the highest priority targets.' What is more, destruction of industrial capacity from such 'smaller' attacks ranges from 60 to over 80 per cent, while casualties 'range from 50 to

80 per cent, deaths from 25 to 50 per cent, and injured from 25 to 30 per cent.'

25 per cent of the population of the United States lives in its ten biggest cities. Supposing Washington, D.C., were to be eliminated straight away in a 'general' nuclear war — for the burst of a single one-megaton bomb over the White House would totally destroy reinforced concrete buildings within a radius of one and a half miles. The Pentagon would have been destroyed, so would the State Department, as would the Bureau of the Budget and other government buildings. New York, Boston, Chicago, Los Angeles, and the other five would be in a corresponding state. The fact that Augusta, Richmond, St. Louis might not have been hit would not matter much from the point of view of organized national life in the USA. Would it be any different in the USSR if Moscow and nine other major Soviet cities had been eliminated?

There is little more worth citing from this report, except that the authors recognize that 'the criteria conventionally used for measuring aggregate economic damage significantly *understate* [my italics] the destructiveness of nuclear attacks, since they do not account for either the indirect or the long-term consequences of widespread destruction for both the society and the economy'. It is also admitted that to bring about a corresponding level of destruction in the USSR required only '10 per cent of current US strategic force loadings', in comparison with the 30 per cent of its strategic forces which the USSR would need to satisfy the computer calculations of 'unacceptable damage' in the USA.

There is only one paragraph that need be quoted from a third recent United States report.[17] It too was published in 1979 by the US Arms Control and Disarmament Agency, and is entitled 'The Effects of Nuclear War'. The paragraph comes from the second part of the Report which deals with the effects of 'general nuclear war between the United

States and the Soviet Union'. Having stated that immediate
human fatalities would number between 25 and 100 million,
that 200 of America's largest cities would be destroyed, and
that 90 per cent of America's urban housing would be
destroyed, it goes on to say:

'The first disease problem to be faced after the attack is
the disposal of tens of millions of cadavers from the humans
and animals that were killed in the attack. In this respect
it should be noted that most of the blast and fire victims
will die during or soon after the attack, the victims of
radiation fallout, however, will die over a longer period of
time (a few days to several weeks). The surviving population
in the first 10 years after the attack will have a substantially
increased disease rate due to lowered resistance because of
radiation, general hardship and poor sanitation. In the longer
run there would be an increase in the cancer rate due to
radioactivity and ultra-violet burning.'

In any realistic scenario of a nuclear exchange, all would
happen in, as it were, a flash, in the same way that Hiroshima
and Nagasaki were destroyed, in the same way as sixteen
square miles of Tokyo were wiped out by small fire bombs
in one night in the spring of 1945. We would not be dealing
with the cumulative addition of small foci of destruction
over a period of years, as in the Second World War. We
would not be dealing with the kind of natural disaster that
now commands headlines — an earthquake near Naples, a
hotel fire in Las Vegas, a major aeroplane crash. Were an
all-out nuclear exchange ever to occur, it is in the greatest
degree unlikely that a full account of what had happened
would ever be written.

CHAPTER 3

Deterrent Strategies

'In-language' and jargon have always characterised military life, military thinking and military writing. Nouns are transformed into verbs, verbs spring out of adjectives, and acronyms become part of ordinary speech. It is a linguistic process that may simplify communication, but it all too often ends by confounding reality. Before the Second World War the word 'interdict' had a legal and ecclesiastical connotation to imply the prohibition of some particular action. This is how 'interdict' is still defined in the *Oxford English Dictionary*. In military parlance, however, it means doing something in order to make it difficult for the enemy to do something he might wish to do; for example, to move from one place to another. 'Taking-out an interdiction target in a theatre war' could mean the total destruction, with a nuclear weapon, of a town with, say, a population of 100,000, 200 miles behind the lines, for no reason other than that it happened to be a railway centre. 'Deter' and 'deterrent' are two other words that have taken on special military meaning in recent years. According to the *O.E.D.*, to deter means 'to restrain from acting or proceeding by any consideration of danger or trouble', and a deterrent is something 'which deters'. In the popular mind, however, and, in the words of General Sir John Hackett,[18] in those of 'military dinosaurs' and 'airborne pterodactyls', the word 'deterrent' today means a nuclear weapon. As one who has read book after book, memoir after memoir on the subject, I can well appreciate that the nuclear has become a golden age for writers who wish to obscure reality in a miasma of words, numbers and acronyms.

The concept of mutual deterrence is basically simple. In discharging its responsibility for the security, survival and welfare of the state, every sovereign government must try to deter another government from taking action which it judges to be contrary to the national interests which it is charged to promote and defend. Conversely, a sane government will be deterred from embarking on hostile acts against another country if, in its judgment, such action would entail either a certain or a significant risk that its own people, its economy and its apparatus of state control, would suffer disproportionately more than would be justified by the value of whatever prizes victory might bring. It is axiomatic that no sane government would initiate or permit acts which, in its opinion, might escalate to a level that would trigger 'unacceptable' nuclear retaliation.

That, in its simplest form, is what is implied by the state of mutual deterrence which characterises the relations in the nuclear sphere between the NATO and Warsaw Pact countries. As Harold Macmillan, then the United Kingdom's Prime Minister, put it as far back as 1960[19] it is hardly likely 'that even the most ambitious or the most ruthless statesman would consciously enter upon so unrewarding an adventure' as the destruction of his own country by nuclear weapons. McGeorge Bundy, the Director of the US National Security Council at the beginning of the sixties, tells us[20] that, from the year he started his presidency, President Kennedy held that 'a general nuclear exchange, even at the levels of 1961, would be so great a disaster as to be an unexampled failure of statesmanship'.

But the concept of nuclear deterrence did not start in so simple a form, nor, the way events are moving, will it end like that. The story begins with the devastation of Hiroshima and Nagasaki in 1945. This final act of the Second

World War revealed that the Americans could make weapons of destruction that were thousands of times more fearful than any that had been known before. Then, three years before the United Kingdom exploded its own first atomic weapon, the Russians demonstrated that they, too, knew the secret of 'The Bomb'. That was in 1949, just about the time when conditions in Europe, and particularly the extension of the sphere of Soviet domination, had led to the formation of NATO as a defensive alliance whose purpose was to prevent the USSR extending still further the geographical area over which it held political sway.

For a time the West believed that it enjoyed an advantage in nuclear weapons, and that its air forces were far more powerful than the Soviet Union's. So in 1954, John Foster Dulles,[21] then the American Secretary of State, proclaimed the doctrine of 'massive retaliation', that is, that in order to deter or counter aggression, the US would 'depend primarily upon a great capacity to retaliate instantly by means and at places of its own choosing'. These were bold words for, almost simultaneously, the grim threat of nuclear retaliation on the American homeland started to become apparent.

This was when the scene underwent a quantum-like transformation. The Soviet Union demonstrated that it could deliver nuclear warheads not only by aircraft, but also by means of inter-continental ballistic missiles. This gave a new twist to the arms race, as the United States accelerated its work in the same field of armaments. Slowly the realisation grew that were the West, and in particular the United States, to use nuclear weapons against the Soviet homeland, the Russians would undoubtedly retaliate in kind, however much smaller in numerical terms their nuclear armoury was at the time. The concept of mutual strategic deterrence then became clear, and with it the belief that since neither side knew whether the other would be the first to unleash a nuclear war, it was essential that both developed the means whereby they could retaliate, whatever the damage they had suffered from what became known as 'a first strike' from the other side. A retaliatory nuclear force had to be 'invulnerable', a term probably first used in this connection by Sir Winston Churchill in 1955.[22] Various techniques were developed to achieve this end.

Paranoia then started to take over, masked by figures of numbers of warheads and delivery systems which, for most people, completely obscured the facts of the destruction that could already be wreaked by just a few nuclear bombs. A few politicians recognised the danger. From 1959 onwards Harold Macmillan fought passionately and valiantly, but in vain, to bring the nuclear arms race to an end. He wanted a ban on all further nuclear testing. At the end of 1960 John F. Kennedy succeeded Eisenhower as President of the United States, and Robert McNamara, then head of the Ford motor company, overnight became his Secretary of Defense, taking over what for him was a new and vastly bigger responsibility. He quickly realised that if Soviet military units were to intrude into NATO territory, there was little sense in the idea of a massive nuclear attack on the Soviet homeland if the Russians could retaliate in kind by striking at America. The price in terms of the destruction which would result from nuclear retaliation would be too high. Instead, he formulated what he first called a 'full options' policy. This necessitated a build-up of NATO's conventional forces.

At the NATO conference held in Lisbon in 1952, force levels had been set for the alliance at 96 divisions, partly in order to obviate the danger of a nuclear war by making it possible to offer a conventional defence to a Soviet attack. But by 1954 it had become apparent that these divisions were never going to materialise, and the NATO Council decided that 'tactical nuclear weapons' should be used to redress any disparity in numbers of men that might occur in a war between the West and the USSR. McNamara's 'full options' policy would comprehend 'graduated nuclear deterrence'.

Simultaneously the heavily-pressed Secretary of Defense had to go on adding flesh to the bones of the concept of mutual strategic nuclear deterrence. Each of the three armed Services wanted the honour of deterring the USSR. McNamara accordingly had to agree a level for the size of the American nuclear forces that could be relied upon to constitute a sufficient threat to the USSR to deter the latter from any nuclear action which would be a direct threat to the USA.

Firm doctrines usually based on arbitrary and theoretical criteria are part of the rule-book of military teaching. At the beginning of the Second World War there were people who, basing their ideas on exaggerated accounts of what had happened in the Spanish Civil War, proclaimed that one German bomb, that is to say a conventional bomb, would flatten a square mile of London. The Royal Air Force may not have believed in such exaggeration, but it certainly vastly overestimated its own powers of destruction and its ability to find its targets. The British Ordnance Board, a venerable body which began in the 15th century, and of which I became an Associate Member in 1947, adhered at the beginning of the Second World War to an arbitrary rule of thumb that only those fragments of an exploding shell or grenade which could penetrate an inch of wood should be regarded as wounding or lethal. Scientific tests were to show later that this criterion enormously underestimated a fragmenting missile's wounding power.[10]

But who it was who set the numerical criterion for 'assured nuclear destruction', later to become 'mutually assured destruction' or MAD, and who it was who persuaded McNamara to accept the criterion, I do not know. What was called for was the power to eliminate a quarter of the Soviet Union's population and to destroy half of its industrial capacity. This, it was estimated, could be done by wiping out the 200 largest cities of the USSR, which together are the home of a third of the country's population. By one of those fortunate coincidences, it transpired that this arbitrary measure of destruction accorded with the level of nuclear armaments whose production had already been planned. In other words, McNamara felt himself bound to put his stamp of approval on what was already in train, presumably in the hopes that by so doing America's nuclear build-up would come to an end. That it did not is clear from the figures for the present size of the nuclear armouries of the super-powers as published during the course of the SALT II negotiations. Between them, the two sides will be allowed to deploy more than 10,000 warheads which could be delivered in a 'strategic' nuclear exchange. In addition, they dispose three, four times as many 'tactical' and 'theatre' nuclear weapons.

Even though the SALT II Treaty that was signed by President Carter has not been ratified by the American Senate, there is no reason to suppose that either side has yet contravened what was agreed about these numbers. They are well in excess of what either side would need were it ever to initiate what has been called 'a spasm of mutual annihilation'.

Soon after McNamara took over as Secretary of Defense, one of his more cynical Assistant Secretaries 'explained' the position to me in this way. 'Don't you see?' he asked. 'First we need enough Minutemen to be sure that we destroy all those Russian cities. Then we need Polaris missiles to follow in order to tear up the foundations to a depth of ten feet, maybe helped by Skybolt' (he happened to believe that Skybolt was a technically ridiculous concept). 'Then, when all Russia is silent, and when no air defences are left, we want waves of aircraft to drop enough bombs to tear the whole place up down to a depth of forty feet to prevent the Martians recolonising the country. And to hell with the fallout.' It was not long before he retired from his post in the Pentagon.

When all this was happening, a few of us were arguing for what we regarded as a more reasonable strategic nuclear policy: the concept of 'minimal deterrence'. It seemed to us inconceivable that in a rational world any country would try to further some aggressive aim if the risk were the total destruction of its own capital city, let alone that of its ten largest cities. This argument got nowhere with our United States colleagues. By 1962 the build-up of the American nuclear forces and, correspondingly, those of the Soviet Union, had already gone well beyond the rational requirements of any mutual deterrent threat. Not only did the build-up never stop, it has, as I have indicated, surpassed any reasonable level. This fact now seems to be recognised in so far as the call for a balanced reduction of forces is today heard on both sides of the Iron Curtain. I shall return later to the question of a 'balanced' reduction.

Ignorance, mutual suspicion, the belief that more destructive power implies greater military security, and the simple difficulty of reducing the momentum which drives an arms race in which thousands are engaged, were the reasons why the two sides did not get together before 1970 to consider how to stop the process. If it is ever negotiated, a curb will still leave enough in both armouries to blow the USA, Europe and the USSR apart. First as Assistant to the President for National Security Affairs and then as Secretary of State, Henry Kissinger had sufficient authority to cry 'enough is enough', that the idea of nuclear superiority no longer made sense.[23] The cry could have been uttered years sooner without any detriment to the security of either side. Unfortunately, the concept of deterrence has always been too vague for definition in terms of units of destruction.

Once the numbers game took over, reason flew out of the window.

Indeed, the concept of deterrence is so vague that ever since 1946 the impression has grown that the Western powers have deterred the Soviet Union from pursuing aggressive plans because of the fear of unacceptable nuclear punishment from the strategic nuclear forces of the West. It is because this belief is now so much part of accepted dogma that, if a presumed intention of the USSR which was, or is, contrary to the West's political interests does not materialise, we conclude that it did not do so because the USSR feared a nuclear onslaught. As the years pass, we run the risk of not asking ourselves whether some presumed hostile intention really existed in the form we supposed. Inevitably the concept of strategic nuclear deterrence becomes an umbrella which covers unsupported as well as supported estimates of the intentions of the other side.

History, of course, does suggest that on occasion both sides have witheld from action for fear of the consequences of a possible nuclear exchange. In the Cuban incident, the Russians presumably withdrew because of this fear. But the fact that the Soviet leaders ever began the operation would suggest that at the time they judged that there was in fact no significant risk of 'unacceptable' retaliation. What would have happened had they not withdrawn their missiles from Cuba is anyone's guess. Correspondingly, the suppression by the Soviet Union of the Hungarian revolt occurred in spite of the violent feelings the action provoked in the West, and in spite also of the West's enormous strategic nuclear striking power. Here the West appeared unready to risk a nuclear war to further what was clearly regarded to be its political interest. Fortunately there are no experiments that either side would be prepared to undertake in order to determine the validity of the belief in the deterrent value of strategic nuclear weapons. Any experiment would cost millions of lives.

A retaliatory force obviously has to look credible, has to look real. If only one side had nuclear weapons, an opponent would be at its mercy. For a state of mutual deterrence to be stable, there has to be some equality of degree of threat above some indefinable level. Clearly, too, to be credible, nuclear forces have to be, or have to seem to be, invulnerable to a 'first strike', by which one means that if one side were to decide to strike at the other without warning, it should not be able to destroy all of its opponent's retaliatory forces. In the framework of deterrent theory, enough should be certain to remain to deter even the idea of a first strike. That is the prescribed reason why both the United States and the USSR maintain a triad of forces: land-based missiles, a force of missile-carrying submarines, and long-range aircraft. If it were possible to eliminate any one of the three arms of strategic deterrence, a possibility to which I shall return, but which I would discount since it has only an illusory political significance, the remaining two, or even one, should be able to threaten 'unacceptable' retaliation.

In spite of the excessive strength of the nuclear armouries of the two sides, and because of the chronic climate of world-wide international unrest, and particularly of the enduring suspicion that prevails between the USA and the USSR, both sides are fearful lest the other gain some advantage in the nuclear arms race. Like their American opposite numbers, the Soviet leaders listened, for example, to the exaggerated claims of their research and development chiefs that an anti-ballistic missile (ABM) system could be devised which would destroy incoming enemy missiles either in outer space or after they had re-entered the earth's atmosphere. Khrushchev boasted that the Russians had it in their power 'to hit a fly in space'. Technical men on both sides have worked feverishly to develop such a system, with complicated radars linked to computer-communication networks and then to batteries of nuclear-armed missiles which would be launched instantaneously into automatically calculated ballistic paths to meet incoming enemy warheads. At the same time, other technical teams focused their efforts on means whereby ABM systems could be defeated. They designed decoys to be carried in the terminal stage of a ballistic missile to confuse the anti-ballistic missile radars. The decoys would be released at the same time as the nuclear warheads, making it difficult, or even impossible for the defending radar systems to differentiate the right objects to track and destroy in flight. But the whole thing was a mirage.

Because these matters are never kept completely secret in the United States, a spirited public debate was stimulated in the late sixties between those technical men who, in spite of one costly failure after another, still claimed that it was possible to devise an effective ABM system, and those who said it was not. Billions of dollars had been spent. In 1967, when ABM fever was at its most acute, and with strong pressure from many quarters for the continued development and then deployment, of a system of defences against missiles, President Johnson summoned not only Dr Don Hornig, his chief Science Adviser, and the Joint Chiefs of Staff, but also the three past presidential Science Advisers, Dr James Killian, Dr George Kistiakowsky, and Dr Jerome Wiesner, as well as the last three Directors of Defense Research and Engineering in the Pentagon: Dr Herbert York, Dr Harold Brown, and Dr John Foster. York describes[24] how the discussion led the President to put two simple questions about a defence system against a possible Russian missile attack: 'Will it work and should it be deployed?'. All present agreed that the answers were No. For what the President wanted to know was whether it was possible to devise a defence which could be relied upon to destroy *all* incoming warheads. It was not sufficient to destroy, say, one in every two, since if only one warhead got through, it would be enough to destroy Washington.

Once both sides were ready to admit the technical and functional futility of work on ABMs, work which could only 'destabilise' the state of mutual deterrence, the first of the SALT talks was embarked upon. Agreement was reached in 1972, by which time Nixon was President and Kissinger in action. Work on the main ABM deployment programmes in the USA and the USSR was then halted. But R and D on ABMs nonetheless continued. It still continues, despite the irrefutable logic of the technical argument that no ABM system could ever be devised that would provide either side with a guarantee that it could escape disaster in a nuclear exchange. However many incoming missiles might be destroyed in the course of their ballistic path, however many bombers might be brought down, enough would still get through to kill millions, to bring organised life to an end, and to nullify organised resistance — and this regardless of fallout from such warheads as might be destroyed in the air. As the British Government's White Paper on Defence put it as long ago as 1957,[25] there are no means of protecting the population against the consequences of nuclear attack. There are none today, when the scale of attack that could be envisaged is at least a hundred times greater than it was twenty years ago. This has become all too clear in the light of the recent studies that have been made of the effects of nuclear attacks on centres of population to which I referred in Chapter 2. One should not be surprised that the newly-elected Greater London Council decided last year to stop diverting resources to plans to deal with the effects of a possible nuclear attack, describing them as a 'farce, a cruel deception, and a waste of money'.[26]

Today we hear talk of laser and charged-particle beam

weapons being developed for deployment on space vehicles to destroy nuclear-headed ballistic missiles in space. Headlines tell us that the space shuttle which the Americans have developed is 'crucial to the future of warfare'. Enthusiasts both in the USA and USSR may well have managed to persuade their paymasters that such ideas are worth the expenditure of vast resources, but there are doubters, probably on both sides of the Iron Curtain. To cite one example, the concept of charged-particle beam weapons has been studied by a highly competent team of physicists[27] at the Massachusetts Institute of Technology (MIT) and their conclusion is that not only are there sound scientific reasons why such systems could not work, but that even if orbiting space vehicles carrying the necessary machinery to generate laser or other beams could be devised, it would be even easier to develop relatively inexpensive counter-measures by which they could be neutralised or destroyed.

But here again it is the political issue that is all-important — not the technical. President Johnson wanted to know whether an ABM system could work. He was neither a physicist nor an engineer. Obviously, if a manned or an unmanned vehicle can be landed within a few feet of a specified point on the surface of the moon, it follows that a combination of Newtonian mechanics, superb computers, perfectly operating radar, plus the associated tracking and firing systems, should make Khrushchev's boast about hitting a fly in space a theoretical possibility. That, however, is not the point. What matters is whether an ABM system could be devised which would give a country's political leader — its commander in chief — the assurance that nuclear fire from the enemy would not be able to destroy his vital cities — Washington, Moscow, London, Paris, and so on. The answer President Johnson was given was No, and in my view the answer will always be No, for the good and simple reason that in any theoretical nuclear scenario it will always be possible to saturate an ABM system with an avalanche of missiles, not to mention strike those targets which may not be protected. What would it matter if some nuclear warheads were destroyed before they hit their targets if in the meantime a few shots had got through to eliminate Washington, D.C., or Chicago, or New York — Moscow, Leningrad, or Kiev?

Today the US strategy of assured or mutually assured destruction has, in theory, been supplanted by what the nuclear theorists know as PD 59 — Presidential Directive 59. This was issued by President Carter in 1979, and it is the general understanding that in it he declared that instead of retaliating against a Soviet nuclear attack by an onslaught on Soviet cities, the Americans would destroy Soviet military targets — missile sites, submarine depots, armament stores, command centres, and so on. PD 59, in short, proclaims what in the jargon is called 'counterforce' strategy, as opposed to a 'countervalue' strategy, the latter being a euphemism for a policy which defines cities as prime targets. PD 59 would therefore be a policy which in theory offered more 'options' than one which led immediately to the destruction of the Western world, including the USSR.

In this sense the new directive is a reflection of McNamara's transformation of 'massive retaliation' into a 'full options' and then 'flexible response' policy for NATO.

In view of the enormous size of the nuclear armouries of the USA and the USSR, one dare not lose sight of the fact that from the operational point of view there is practically no difference, apart from the verbal one, between what is now called counterforce and what is termed countervalue. Henry Kissinger justified the development of MIRVed missiles by the United States because MIRVs were going to be accurate enough to 'take out' Soviet military targets, so that, on paper at least, cities would be spared. He therefore regarded the affirmation of a counterforce strategy as more 'humane' than one based upon 'assured destruction'. So, at the time of the SALT II talks, it was only 'logical' for the Americans to press on with the MIRV systems which they had already developed, and for which it was appropriate to formulate a different policy, especially as it was argued that the Russians were fairly advanced in the development of their own accurate MIRVed missiles. If the Russians were to develop the capacity to threaten or, worse, to embark upon, a first strike against the American nuclear forces, the Americans clearly could not forgo what they had already achieved technically. Moreover, there was another consideration. For the total weight it could carry, a MIRVed ballistic missile could wreak more destruction than a ballistic missile carrying the same 'throw-weight' in one nuclear charge — for from this point of view, the greater the number of nuclear packets in the total explosive charge the better. From the Soviet point of view, the Americans were not going to abandon MIRV developments. Why should they? The fact that a 'counterforce' policy could not deprive either side of so much of its total retaliatory forces — for example, ballistic missile submarines would be immune to a counterforce strike — as to make any meaningful difference to the prospective levels of retribution, was immaterial in the context of a technological race.

The earlier views expressed by Henry Kissinger about 'counterforce' seem to be the conventional wisdom embodied in PD 59. The belief now is that were the state of deterrence to break down, a Soviet nuclear offensive would begin with an assault on American fixed missile sites, with the USA then striking at corresponding military targets in the USSR. Theoretically that would then leave both sides with their missile submarines and long-range aircraft intact.

But it is inevitable, too, that were military installations rather than cities to become the objectives of nuclear attack, millions, even tens of millions, of civilians would nonetheless be killed, whatever the number of missile sites, airfields, armament plants, ports, and so on that would be destroyed. As I have said, statements of the accuracy of missile strikes are given in terms of the acronym CEP (circular error probable), i.e. the radius of a circle within which fifty per cent of strikes should fall. Even if one were to assume that navigational, homing and all the other devices worked perfectly, the fifty per cent outside the magic circle would not necessarily have a normal distribution; that is to say, the strikes falling off in regular fashion with increasing distance from the pre-ordained target. Moreover, whatever the accuracy with which they could be delivered, nuclear weapons still have an enormous area of effect relative to the precise 'military' targets at which the supposed counterforce strikes would be aimed. And, were a nuclear exchange ever to be embarked upon, it seems inevitable that the side which felt it was losing would use elements of its nuclear armoury against the enemy's centres of population.

When one looks further, the difference between a policy of 'assured destruction' on the one hand, and that of counterforce or PD 59, becomes even more verbal and illusory. London is a major command centre. Most government buildings, including the Ministry of Defence, are in, or close to, Whitehall. These would obviously be a 'counterforce' target for the Soviet Union. A single megaton bomb would destroy them all, and at the same time remove Westminster Abbey, Buckingham Palace, Waterloo Station, St Thomas's and the Westminster Hospitals, and everything within a two-mile radius of No. 10 Downing Street. Washington is the central command centre of the United States, and Moscow that of the USSR. There is Bonn and there is Paris. Who would be left to ask whether, given the outbreak of nuclear hostilities, these great cities had been effaced because they had had a place in one or another list of targets?

McGeorge Bundy, who played so big a part in the development of America's nuclear strategy, recently had this to say:[20]

'We Americans know from the repeated declarations of our senior military leaders that our own strategic plans have always been focussed mainly on military targets, but we also know from a recent unclassified report that a retaliatory strategic strike on just such targets would put some sixty warheads on Moscow. There may be room for argument about this "military" target or that one, but niceties of targeting doctrine do not make the weapons themselves discriminating.'

The play is one of words, not of realities. The reality is that as nuclear warheads are turned out, they are assigned to specific targets. And there are already more than enough warheads on both sides to deal with whatever number of targets are regarded as relevant to a deterrent strategy. I have always held, and I repeat, that no rational political leader could ever conceive that any political prize was worth the risk of the destruction of the ten major cities of his country. What is more, those who should know and who have declared themselves, do not believe that any nuclear exchange could be 'contained'. In 1980, General Richard H. Ellis, the Director of America's Joint Strategic Target Planning Staff, and the present head of America's Strategic Air Command, explained[28] the merits of America's 'flexible' targeting policy, and ended his paper by quoting the following lines from the Annual Report to Congress for the Federal Year 1981 that was presented by Dr Harold Brown, then the Secretary of Defense.

'Our targeting plan allows sufficient flexibility to selectively employ nuclear weapons as the situation dictates.

Such a capability, and this degree of flexibility, we have believed for some years, would enable us to:

— prevent an enemy from achieving any meaningful advantage;

— inflict higher costs on him than the value he might expect to gain from partial or full-scale attacks on the United States and its allies; and

— leave open the possibility of ending an exchange before the worst escalation and damage had occurred, even if avoiding escalation to mutual destruction is not likely.'

The final ten words of this statement are those that matter.

When one dismisses the mumbo-jumbo of the theorists, or some of the abstractions that have grown up in discussions of nuclear weapons, the basic strategic facts of our nuclear age are thus quite simple.

First, nuclear weapons exist and cannot be brushed aside. They are at present deployed in thousands by both the United States and the USSR and, to a much smaller extent, by the United Kingdom. France is also an operational nuclear power, and China might well be.

Second, the two super-powers have shown by their actions that while they recognise the extreme danger which these weapons imply to themselves as well as to their enemies, neither is prepared to take any step which they think might give the other a potential advantage in the nuclear field, so long as there is no settlement of the political differences which separate the Western from the Eastern bloc of nations. Because of the fear that the balance of strategic deterrence might be disrupted, with the advantage dramatically moving to one or other side, both spend vast sums in trying to find a technical solution to the intractable problem which a defence against ballistic missiles implies. Correspondingly, as has been argued for years by those who know the facts, for example Wiesner and York,[29] there is no reason to suppose that any further elaboration of nuclear weapons could significantly improve the military security or strength of either of the two super-powers.

CHAPTER 4

Fighting
with Nuclear Weapons

Even before Mr McNamara had substituted his 'full options' and then renamed 'flexible response' policy for Foster Dulles's 1954 explicit policy of 'massive retaliation', the Americans, and no doubt the Russians, had started to design and develop what were called small or tactical nuclear weapons for presumed use in field warfare. In the early fifties, all manner of warhead developments were being thought up, following hard on the free-falling bombs which were the first that both sides (and the UK) had made. Small kiloton rockets, nuclear shells and mines, even torpedoes, were being designed. My own knowledge of what was happening was indirect, and I was then privy to no secrets about warheads, either British or American. But it was known that during the early part of the Second World War I had made a study of the anti-personnel effects of the blast from conventional bombs. I was therefore called in as a 'consultant' by a team of American medical men in New Mexico (one an old pupil of mine) who had been given a contract to find out whether the blast or shock wave from a nuclear explosion, which differs in some physical 'parameters' from that set up by a chemical explosive, also had different anti-personnel effects. The American Services were then battling between themselves as to who should develop rockets, and what rockets. The late Wernher von Braun, the leader of the German team that during the

Second World War developed the V2 at Peenemunde, and who became an American citizen after the war, was a pawn in this game. He was one of several space scientists whom I met when helping to agree a programme of blast research. The fact is that before the strategists or formulators of military policy had even uttered a word, the idea that nuclear armaments could be used, given that a war broke out in NATO Europe, had taken firm shape in the minds of the technical people, and implicit with it went the belief that were a few nuclear weapons to be exploded in a land battle, in association with a massive nuclear strike against the Soviet Union, the mainland of Europe would be spared the devastation and horrors of yet another prolonged war.

In short, the notion that tactical nuclear weapons could be used as 'artillery' to compensate for inferior numbers of men did not evolve as a result of any precise analysis. It was just a reasonable hope in the days when the West manifestly had a bigger nuclear arsenal than the USSR. Later, when it had become clear that the Western advantage was far from overwhelming, there arose a school of thought which held that the use of tactical nuclear weapons would nonetheless be able to compensate for a numerical inferiority in conventional forces. So by 1954 NATO had begun to plan for what is now a vast nuclear armoury which was to be used not only by tactical aircraft, but also by ground forces, with field launchers deployed at divisional level (and even below), and with control ostensibly vested in the Supreme Allied Commander of the Allied Forces in Europe (SACEUR), with powers of delegation going all the way down to the level of army corps. Ever since the early 1960s, when McNamara first announced the figure, this 'tactical' armoury has been consistently stated to comprise 7,000 warheads.

So far as I understand it, the first theoretical exposition of the concept that small nuclear weapons could and should be used in field warfare was that of Kissinger in 1957. In 1960 he qualified his position in a book called *The Necessity for Choice*[30] — in particular in a chapter entitled 'Limited War — A Reappraisal', in which he fully recognised the danger that a 'limited' war would, in all likelihood, quickly escalate to an all-out nuclear exchange and so to mutual destruction. In what was essentially a theoretical and somewhat ambivalent analysis, he presented both sides of the argument, but in an unrealistic way which suggested that a field war unfolds in steps agreed beforehand in some rational way by the participants. But it did lead him to the conclusion that even by 1960 'the notion that nuclear weapons can substitute for numerical inferiority' had lost 'a great deal of its validity'. In his 1960 book he also condemned as 'fallacious or exaggerated' the idea that the NATO powers could not muster sufficient conventional strength to counter a Soviet attack. As he put it, 'a nuclear defense becomes the *last* and not the *only* recourse.'

In the same year, Basil Liddell Hart published an even more impressive, but now equally forgotten, book entitled *Deterrent or Defence*.[31] In it he argued that were 'small' nuclear weapons used to stop advancing troops, the result would most likely be escalation to the use of H-bombs, 'precipitating an illimitable and suicidal H-bomb devastation of countries and cities'. The concepts of 'victory' and 'total war' had become 'totally absurd' now that these weapons existed. 'Nuclear parity', he wrote, 'leads to nuclear nullity — because the suicidal boomerang result of using such weapons induces strategic sterility'. And in referring to 'the problem of tactical atomic weapons', he added 'it would be better if such weapons had never been introduced' because 'the use of such weapons might all too easily spread into all-out war. We need to develop a new system for higher control that will combine restraining power with rapidity, and political with military judgement in any decision to use them. It is too risky to leave the decision to military commanders. For they will always tend to use every weapon available if it looks likely that their troops will be overrun. In that immediate concern they tend to lose sight of wider issues. By taking the narrow view they have often in the past marred the aims of higher policy. Now, they could wreck the world.'

Neither Kissinger's nor Liddell Hart's theoretical analyses had much effect on what has happened since. Nor, until recently, did a series of more empirical studies which, as Chief Scientific Adviser to the British Minister of Defence, I had set in hand early in 1960, and the results of which I soon after discussed with a group of senior United States defence and nuclear scientists. These studies formed the basis of the paper which I presented to the annual meeting of the NATO Commanders in the summer of 1961, and which was later published. (see p.xi)[1]

The analysis dealt specifically with the central front along which NATO forces face those of the Warsaw Pact powers. In the light of the prevailing strategy, it presupposed that there would be no political inhibitions to the use of nuclear weapons for, as Field Marshal Montgomery, then the Deputy to the Supreme Commander had put it[32], 'I want to make it absolutely clear that we at SHAPE are basing all our operational planning on using atomic and thermo-nuclear weapons in our defence. With us it is no longer: "They may possibly be used." It is very definitely: "They will be used, if we are attacked".' My studies also presupposed that hostilities would start with a deliberate advance by Soviet troops into Western Germany (this assumption is a constant feature in all the war-games which 'our side' plays, and in all exercises which it practises, in the same way as, in Soviet exercises, the NATO powers are the aggressors).

In the realisation that nuclear weapons might be used in

any part of the area over which our forces were deployed, the Russians as well as ourselves would have necessarily deployed in depth, and in such a way that no more than one 'unit' would, on average, be vulnerable to a nuclear strike. Such units, called 'minor units' at the time I did my analysis, would normally consist of a company of infantry, a squadron of tanks, a battery of artillery, or some combination of these of roughly equivalent size — in all a unit of around a hundred men and their equipment. This tactical necessity would have immediately imposed a need for great mobility and highly sophisticated communications.

Being the attackers in this now classical scenario, the Warsaw Pact forces would have clearly mustered in great strength. If, as is always assumed, they outnumbered the defending NATO forces, and these were going to resort to nuclear fire in order to hold the attack, then in theory the NATO defenders would have had to be ready to fire as many nuclear weapons as would be necessary to reduce the attacking forces to the number of minor units that they could hold and then throw back. Clearly an offensive might be held in this way for a short time. On the other hand, given that the attacking force returned the nuclear fire, which would be the expected response, and in spite of the fact that the defenders would normally be less vulnerably disposed than the attackers, the battle in theory would in the end have to go to the attacking side, given that it went on deploying its presumed greater number of units.

It is military doctrine to assume an offensive: defensive force ratio of about 3:1. With 200 minor units ('teeth-arms') to a British corps (which was the 'drill' when these analyses were made), it was easy to calculate that hundreds of nuclear weapons would inevitably be fired in the area of battle if both sides were to use them. But the numbers of nuclear weapons that would be fired in a battle on, say, a corps front would cause so much physical damage (regardless of the numbers of actual military casualties) as to render the idea of mobile or any other form of warfare meaningless. The damage in the battlefield area would be as great as would occur in an exchange of strategic nuclear weapons.

These conventional propositions and their theoretical implications were tested in practical war-games that were played by experienced army divisional commanders. It turned out that the average 'pay-off' for the NATO defenders was slightly more than one nuclear strike to dispose of one Soviet minor unit, and for the Russians, somewhere between one and two strikes to eliminate one minor unit of the better entrenched NATO defenders. The picture that emerged from a series of tests was fairly consistent. In a nuclear battle on NATO territory, between 200 and 250 nuclear 'strikes' of average yield 20 kt would be exploded in the space of a few days in an area no more than 50 by 30 miles (80×50 km). The effect would have been indescribable, and meaningless from the point of view of any continuing battle between opposing armies. In one war game in which it was assumed that only the defending British forces used nuclear weapons, but in which the Russians for some reason or other refrained from using them, the detonation of sixty nuclear weapons of average yield 15.6 kt still failed to prevent the Russians from crossing the River Weser in force. They were, however, held in another war game, in which the Russians again did not fire nuclear weapons, but when our troops used 130 nuclear weapons.

Needless to say, were the Soviet Union ever to launch an attack against the NATO front, it would not be just one British army corps that would be engaged. In a real situation, nuclear battles of the kind I have described would be taking place in adjacent corps areas, at the same time as aircraft would be striking deep, up to a distance of hundreds of miles, into enemy territory, and very likely into Soviet air-space, in what are now called 'interdiction' attacks on enemy airfields, centres of command and communication, missile-launching sites, supposed nuclear depots, and so on. Even though it was only rational to assume that the Soviet Union would also be making 'interdiction' strikes, it was regarded as bad form to ask to which of our undestroyed airfields our own aircraft would be returning from their deep penetration strikes. The weapons available for such attacks would have yields of scores of kilotons, running into the megaton range.

In another exercise that involved three **NATO** corps in a 10,000 square mile area in which no large towns or cities were 'priority interdiction targets', nuclear weapons were used exclusively against presumed 'military targets'. In this battle, which lasted only a few days, it was assumed that, together, the two sides — although in unequal numbers — delivered no fewer than five hundred, and no more than a thousand, nuclear strikes totalling 20 to 25 megatons. The result was that 3½ million people would have had their homes destroyed if the weapons had been air-burst, and 1½ million if ground-burst. In the former case at least half the people concerned would have been fatally or seriously injured. In the case of the ground-burst weapons, all 1½ million would have been exposed to a lethal radiation hazard, and a further 5 million to serious damage from radiation.

With the speed with which any supposed nuclear battle would be fought, it is out of the question that either side would have the time or resources to deal with the spread of radioactive contamination over an area of hundreds of square miles. Nor, of course, would there be any monitoring of the yield of each enemy strike as a check on the enemy's intentions, so as to reply with weapons of corresponding yield. There are no rules in nuclear or any form of warfare like those which apply in the boxing-ring.

The belief that the neutron or 'clean' bomb could make any difference to what might happen in a nuclear battle on European soil is a total illusion. The idea is that such weapons could help hold up a Soviet armoured advance because radiation would kill tank crews without destroying their vehicles. I have already set out on p.19 some of the practical considerations which argue against this concept. There are others. Both the radius of effect and the yield of any neutron bomb that would make technical sense are known. It would be naïve to assume that the Russians are unaware of the basic facts; indeed, there is a strong rumour that they have not only experimented with, but developed similar warheads. If, therefore, the Soviet Union were to attack in the expectation that they would meet nuclear fire, they would not deploy their armour at the right distances to optimise the effects of, say, a one-kt neutron bomb. That being the obvious military precaution, one needs to ask how many neutron bombs would be needed to knock out a tank. Certainly, on average, more than one. Moreover, radiation would not necessarily kill the crews of tanks immediately. They would continue to advance into, presumably, more neutron bomb fire. But neutron bombs are nuclear weapons. The Russians could hardly be expected not to reply in kind. They would respond not according to some sets of rules about radiation in relation to blast, or about explosive effects generally, agreed beforehand with their enemy. In the heat of the battle they would reply with whatever nuclear weapons they would regard as most useful militarily.

It is not surprising that the alarm which already existed in some member states about NATO's nuclear policy was sharpened by the announcement in August 1981 that the United States was manufacturing and stockpiling 'neutron' warheads. In my view, and contrary to what some commentators have suggested, the main reason for this reaction was not that the Americans have confused the issue by referring to the weapon as a 'bomb' that kills people without destroying buildings or armoured vehicles; by claiming, for some convoluted reason, that it is more humane than other nuclear weapons from the point of view of those civilians who would be 'unlucky' enough to find themselves in a zone of battle. What is more important is that both President Reagan and his Defence Secretary - neither a scientist nor known for his military experience - have helped spread the impression that 'neutron bombs' belong to a new category of weapon totally different from the already horrifying 'atomic' or 'hydrogen' bombs. Had this been their deliberate intention, as opposed probably to a failure to appreciate that the explosion of *any* nuclear weapon leads to the emission of dangerous neutrons, it could not have played better into the hands of the Soviet Union, which condemned the announcement as a deliberate exacerbation of the arms race. This was in keeping with the way the Russians met the NATO decision to station 572 (why 572?) cruise missiles and Pershing II rockets on European soil as an answer to the deployment of the Soviet SS20 missile. As I now see it, the publicity associated with the neutron warhead, in so far as it may encourage the military in the false belief that the weapon could be used without risking all-out nuclear war, could 'lower the nuclear threshold'. But the fact remains that neutron warheads are no more moral or immoral than any other nuclear weapon. Such basic scientific differences as exist between one or other kind of nuclear weaponry are less than those which separate certain kinds of armament normally regarded as conventional.

Both the logic of the situation and the results of war games show that escalation to all-out nuclear war is all but implicit in the concept of fighting a field war with 'tactical' and 'theatre' nuclear weapons. Regardless of the care commanders might imagine they could take to confine damage to military targets, a nuclear battlefield in Europe would be a zone in which towns and villages would have been devastated; in which all but the strongest buildings would have been utterly destroyed; in which roads would have been blocked and bridges made impassable; in which forests would have been razed; in which extensive fires would be raging; and over which vast numbers of casualties would have occurred. In Western Europe the range of effect of single megaton weapons may include more than one big town, and villages are certainly not many kilotons apart.

Nuclear weapons may well be classified as strategic, theatre, and tactical, but these terms are meaningless if the use of one of them may mean the use of any. They can only be judged by their effects. Moreover, the Soviet Union would have no reason to trust any Western assertions about an intention to limit nuclear warfare to the 'battlefield'. If NATO field forces were provided with adequate air support, our aircraft would be attacking targets deeper and deeper into enemy territory. A field commander would tend to use more and more weapons if it became apparent that a previous weight of attack was not having the desired effect of halting the enemy. Once the weapons he used included nuclear warheads, the likelihood is that more would be used. My experience of generals and air marshals in the Second World War agrees with Liddell Hart's observations. It does not lead me to suppose that, if unlimited force were available, less rather than more would be used in order to secure some objective.

There is, of course, no rule which says that a land battle in Europe would immediately 'go nuclear'. But the only conceivable reason why a nuclear battlefield would not escalate to an all-out nuclear exchange would be because both sides simultaneously stopped to consider what the further consequences might be. It is just possible that one side might not reply in kind, say, to a nuclear 'shot across the bows', or to the attempted 'discriminate' use of nuclear weapons, or even to a first strategic strike. But for this to happen command and control, as well as the scope of intelligence and reconnaissance, would for both sides have to be considerably better technically than they now are, at the same time as the psychological reactions of the contestants would have to be the reverse of what has been the pattern in previous wars. Were either side to resort to the use of nuclear weapons, it would do so only in the belief that such action would avert defeat or bring victory. Once that happened, it is ludicrous to suppose that the other side would not respond, even if for the same illusory reason.

The very existence of tactical nuclear weapons is thus the most urgent challenge that has ever been presented to the system whereby military judgment and control have to be exercised. As weapons to deter aggression, they serve a precise purpose; the context of field warfare in which they might actually be used is an entirely different matter. There can be few military targets which are not disproportionately small in relation to the area of effect of the smallest nuclear weapon that might be used against them. Once one goes beyond, say, a yield of 20 kilotons, one is in the 'town-elimination range'. Because of this, valid comparisons cannot be made between the introduction to the military scene of nuclear weapons and, say, the introduction of conventional explosives or poison gases at the time they emerged. There is built into nuclear weapons greater destructive power than is necessary for military purposes, and their secondary, non-military effects overshadow those which relate specifically to their military use.

I do not know what further analyses have been done in recent years by NATO planners, and I know of none that has been published by Soviet planners. But I do know that several have been made by American analysts that confirm the conclusion which I published twenty years ago. Alain Enthoven, who between 1960 and 1969 held many posts in the American Department of Defense, including that of Assistant Secretary of Defense for Systems Analysis, wrote[33] in 1975 that 'in eight years of studying the problem, I never saw a convincing scenario in which such use [of nuclear weapons] would make sense'. He goes on to say: 'Tactical nuclear weapons cannot defend Europe; they can only destroy it. Studies and war games done in the 1960s showed repeatedly that even under the most favorable assumptions about restraint and limitations in yields and targets, between 2 and 20 million Europeans would be killed in a limited tactical nuclear war, with widespread damage to the economy of the affected area, and a high risk of 100 million deaths if the war escalated to attacks on cities. And, because of the vulnerability of key forces, the big advantages to striking first, and the location near cities of many airfields, transportation links, command posts and the like, the likelihood of such escalation would be very high . . . there is no such thing as a two-sided tactical nuclear war in the sense of sustained purposive military operations . . . nobody knows how to fight a tactical nuclear war. Twenty years of effort by many military experts have failed to produce a believable doctrine for tactical nuclear warfare.'

He is right. Five of the seven officers who have held the post of Chief of the Defence Staff in the British military hierarchy since it was established in 1957 (the eighth is now in office) have recently made public statements which accord with the conclusions to which my 1960-61 analyses led. All were also members of the NATO Military Committee, which two of them chaired for some years. There is no need to quote from all their recent public statements. This is what the late Admiral of the Fleet, Lord Mountbatten, Chief of the Defence Staff from 1959 to 1965, said in a much-quoted speech which he delivered in Strasbourg in 1979,[34] a few months before he was murdered. The belief that nuclear weapons 'could be used in field warfare without triggering an all-out nuclear exchange leading to the final holocaust' is 'more and more incredible. I cannot accept the reasons for the belief that any class of nuclear weapons can be categorized in terms of their tactical or strategic purposes. In all sincerity, as a military man I can see no use for any nuclear weapons which would not end in escalation, with consequences that no one can conceive.'

Admiral of the Fleet, Lord Hill-Norton, who was Chief of the Defence Staff from 1971 to 1973, has said[35] that he knows of no informed observer who believes that war-fighting with nuclear weapons is credible. Field Marshal Lord Carver, who succeeded Lord Hill-Norton, agrees.[36] 'It is not a concept which any sensible, responsible, military person now holds that you would fight a war in Europe with tactical or theatre nuclear weapons and thus avoid a strategic nuclear exchange'. Marshal of the RAF, Sir Neil Cameron who as Chief of the Defence Staff preceded the present incumbent, has put on record[37] that he 'agrees 100 per cent' that the 'notion of winning some sort of military success in an exchange of nuclear weapons is unreal ... so-called battlefield nuclear weapons are not means of winning military victories ... the warfighting school of nuclear theorists has lost the argument in the west.'

Leading American military figures now say the same. General A. S. Collins Jr. writes[38] that once a nuclear round is fired in a land battle, 'no one can be sure what will happen, and no one should ignore the fact that control of events passes to the other side'. The General analyses the sequence of likely events, assuming that the first nuclear round has been fired by NATO forces who are about to be over-run and that the enemy — i.e. the Warsaw Pact forces — have replied in kind. His view is that the US military recommendation would then be to strike again 'with all available tactical weapons', concluding that 'once the decision is made at the highest level of government to use tactical nuclear weapons, and release authority is passed down the chain of command, after one or two nuclear interchanges conditions in the land battle area will make control of use questionable.'

General Maxwell Taylor, who ended his military career as Chairman of the US Joint Chiefs of Staff under Kennedy and Johnson, is reported to have expressed similar views,[39] as have other leading American and French military men. In 1962, Helmut Schmidt, now the Chancellor of the Federal Republic of Germany, endorsed the same cautionary view in a book called *Defence or Retaliation*.[40] 'The theory of the inevitability of nuclear defence is fatally wrong ... Defence against a non-nuclear aggression in Europe with the aid of tactical nuclear weapons, even in the unlikely event of both sides keeping within bounds and avoiding the upward acceleration of weapons, would most probably mean the extensive destruction of Europe and, at all events, of Germany. In the interest of maintaining the substance of Europe and particularly of Germany, NATO must therefore have troops and weapons on a scale ample to make non-nuclear aggression appear hopeless, and sufficient in an emergency to force one of two courses on the aggressor — to halt or to extend the conflict.'

Yet despite all the authoritative evidence and opinion indicating the extreme improbability that a tactical or theatre nuclear war could be contained, NATO has never renounced the publicly-declared doctrine of 'first use'; that is to say that if Warsaw Pact forces were to attack and over-run NATO positions, the Western Alliance would initiate the use of nuclear weapons. It is argued that this is not a counsel of despair, but a reasonable response to Soviet military doctrine that a field war in which nuclear weapons are used can not only be fought but can also be won. The authority usually cited for this belief is the late Marshal Sokolovskii, the author of a massive tome on *Military*

Strategy,[41] in which one reads statements such as 'the Armed Forces of the Soviet Union and the other socialist countries must be prepared above all to wage war under conditions of the mass use of nuclear weapons by both belligerent parties. Therefore, the correct and profoundly scientific solution of all the questions related to the preparation and waging of just such a war must be regarded as the main task of the theory of military strategy and strategic leadership.'

But Sokolovskii harboured no illusions that a nuclear war could be contained, and he was aware of the limitless destructive power of nuclear weapons. 'The logic of war', he wrote, 'is such that if a war is unleashed by the aggressive circles of the United States, it will immediately be transferred to the territory of the United States of America. All weapons: ICBMs, missiles from submarines, and other strategic weapons, will be used in this military conflict.' The consequences, as spelt out by Sokolovskii, are plain:

'The losses in a world nuclear war will not only be suffered by the USA and their NATO allies, but also by the socialistic countries. The logic of a world nuclear war is such that in the sphere of its effect would fall an overwhelming majority of the world's states. As a result of a war many hundreds of millions of people would perish, and most of those remaining alive, in one respect or another, would be subject to radioactive contamination.'

Bernard Brodie, a political scientist who was among the first writers to consider critically[42] what the advent of nuclear weapons implied for world politics and military strategy, has more recently[43] taken to task certain of the foremost American hard-liners, who use the argument that the Russians believe they can win a nuclear war in order to promote the complementary view that America could. He cites Professor Pipes, a professor of Russian History at Harvard University, and well-known for his belligerent attitude, as one of the main protagonists of this view. (Before Professor Pipes became a member of the staff of the National Security Council, he is reported as having struck fear in some presidential circles by proclaiming that one of the new administration's first aims should be the elimination of communism from the Soviet Union.) Brodie refers to a recent article by Professor Pipes entitled 'Why the Soviet Union thinks it could fight and win a nuclear war', and then goes on to say, 'The "why" in the title of Mr Pipes' article preempts the prior question *whether* some entity called the Soviet Union thinks as he says it does. The appropriate question is: *who* in the Soviet Union thinks they can fight and win a nuclear war? The article tells us that it is some Soviet generals who think so, not a single political leader being mentioned. One could at this point dismiss the issue by remarking that there are also plenty of US generals who think that the United States could fight and win a nuclear war and are even willing to give a definition for the word "win", though few of us would be comfortable with that definition.'

At a recent small international meeting, I had the opportunity to discuss the point with General Mikhail Milshtein, a Soviet general and military spokesman who has represented the USSR in the SALT negotiations and in other disarmament talks. He found my questions surprising. 'What are your soldiers taught?', he asked, 'that the weapons with which they are furnished are no good, and that they should lay down their arms and go home? The men at the top in the USSR understand the incredible dangers just as much as your leaders do. No one can win with nuclear weapons.' In an interview recorded in the *New York Times* of 28th August 1980, General Milshtein gave the Soviet view as follows: 'We believe that nuclear war will bring no advantage to anyone and may even lead to the end of civilisation. And the end of civilisation can hardly be called victory. Our doctrine regards nuclear weapons as something that must never be used. They are not an instrument for waging war in any rational sense. They are not weapons with which one can achieve foreign policy goals. But if we are forced to use them, in reply to their first use by an aggressor, we shall use them, with all their consequence, for the punishment of the aggressor.'

In this statement General Milshtein was echoing what Khrushchev and Brezhnev have also said about nuclear weapons. Even if any Soviet general believed that a nuclear war could be won, the belief would still be nonsense.

One might well ask how it is that so many 'top' British military leaders when out of office have expressed views about tactical or theatre nuclear weapons which are so much at variance with the armament programmes and tactical teaching which they presumably endorsed when they were in command? My first answer would be that although in command, they were in no position to reverse a trend in the process of development and deployment of nuclear weapons which derives its momentum not from any formulation of well thought-out operational requirements, but from the minds of enthusiastic technicians plying their trade in the weapons laboratories. My second would be that military teaching cannot run foul of the need for discipline. Where it is the habit of the scientist to question, it is that of the soldier to obey. Only those who have belonged to the armed services in the field, or who have worked with them, can appreciate just how vital this power of command and authority is to the whole hierarchy of military organisation. Discipline of this kind would be impossible in an organisation which was subject to the doubts that are brought about by rapid change, and particularly by the winds of technological change. This is as true of the military machine in peace as it is in war. Each level of command accepts the wisdom and authority of the one above. The soldier must have faith in his weapons. Someone, somehow, must make 'the man at the sharp end' believe that the weapons with which he has been provided are at least as good as those the potential enemy has at his disposal.

A third reason is that no military leader could on his own call for the removal of nuclear weapons that are provided for possible use in field warfare when they are also deployed by the potential enemy. Such decisions are in the political sphere, and they have to be symmetrical.

In the irrational world in which we live so precariously, the armoury of 'tactical' nuclear weapons which both sides deploy is regarded as an additional band in the spectrum of mutual deterrence. But the longer this situation lasts, the more hazardous it becomes. For as the years roll on, the concept of nuclear warfare becomes ever more established in tactical teaching, and the danger of the use of nuclear weapons ever greater. Were they to be used, it would not matter whether the first shot was fired by accident or because of tactical doctrine. The end would be the same.

In an article entitled 'The forgotten dimensions of strategy', Professor Michael Howard, who has thought deeply and written much on the strategic problems of today, has observed[44] that 'the interest displayed by Soviet writers in the conduct of such a [nuclear] war, which some writers in the West find so sinister', seemed to him 'no more than common sense ... It is not good enough to say that the strategy of the West is one of deterrence, or even of crisis management. It is the business of the strategist to think what to do if deterrence fails, and if Soviet strategists are doing their job and those in the West are not, it is not for us to complain about them.'

In his view: 'The Western position appears both paradoxical and, quite literally, indefensible, so long as our operational strategy quite explicitly envisages the initiation of a nuclear exchange. The use of theater nuclear weapons within Western Europe, on any scale, will involve agonizing self-inflicted wounds for which our societies are ill-prepared; while their extension to Eastern European territory will invite retaliation against such legitimate military targets as the ports of Hamburg, Antwerp or Portsmouth. . . . The planned emplacement of nuclear weapons in Western Europe capable of matching in range, throw-weight and accuracy those which the Russians have targeted onto that area may be necessary to deter the Soviet Union from initiating such an exchange. But it will not solve the problem so long as the Russians are in a position to secure an operational victory without recourse to nuclear weapons at all. Deterrence works both ways.'

With the risks as they are, it stands to reason that so long as the Western and Warsaw powers remain at odds with each other, the NATO powers will have to deploy conventional forces in sufficient strength to hold any possible Soviet attack, if for no other reason than to allow sufficient time for political mediation. The converse also applies. So long as the Russians believe that the West might be the aggressor, they will deploy conventional forces. There is endless and fruitless argument about the relative conventional strengths of the two sides, and about the nature of the forces which the Soviet Union deploys on the territory of its allies. There are some who argue that the disparity is not as great as others pretend. There are those who declare that such Soviet forces as are deployed in Poland, Czechoslovakia and Eastern Germany are clearly armed not merely to prevent a civil uprising, but as they would be were they to advance against the West.

These arguments are irrelevant to the main threat. Nuclear war would be an unutterable disaster to all sides. If the Soviet Union were to attack, and our response became nuclear, all would be lost. If the reverse were to happen, the end would be the same. There is no alternative to our deploying enough properly armed conventional forces to fight, if it ever becomes necessary, a real war. Armies are not raised in order to initiate a process that within days would destroy most of the advanced countries of the world.

It stands to reason that only conventional forces can provide the flexibility that can negate the disastrous rigidity that is implicit in the concept of the automatic and first use of nuclear weapons. Only such forces can increase the number of 'options' open to the NATO command. Equally, the concept of 'graduated deterrence' — the earlier catch-word which is now replaced by the term 'flexible response', is only a confusing abstraction. As I have said, there are no agreed rules for field warfare in which nuclear weapons might be used. Indeed, it is all but impossible to impart real meaning to the idea of a continuous spectrum of possible responses, ranging from a small conventional defence to a more powerful conventional defence; to conventional def-ence backed by tactical nuclear weapons; and so on to operations escalating into all-out strategic nuclear war. The spectrum consists of two bands: one comprising operations in which nuclear weapons are *not* used, the other, operations in which they are. The separation is imposed not by a graduated series of levels of destructive energy, but by the fact that nuclear weapons have changed the nature of destructive force, and made it limitless in its effects.

When discussing the modernisation of NATO's nuclear armoury in September 1980, Henry Kissinger is reported[45] to have said that the European allies of the United States should not keep asking the USA 'to multiply strategic assurances that we cannot possibly mean or if we do mean, we should not want to execute, because if we execute we risk the destruction of civilization'. No stronger endorse-ment than this could be sought for the paradox enunciated by York and Wiesner in 1964[29] — and which I had stated publicly even earlier — that the continued growth of nuclear arsenals not only fails to increase, but actually decreases, national security.

What was true twenty years ago is even truer today.

CHAPTER 5

Independence

In 1963, the USA, the USSR, and the UK, the only countries which by then had produced and deployed nuclear weapons, attached their signatures to a treaty that banned the further testing of nuclear warheads either in the atmosphere or in the seas. In fairly quick succession more than ninety other nations signified that they would also adhere to the Treaty. France and China abstained. By 1967, when the Non-Proliferation Treaty (NPT) was concluded, there were five nuclear-weapon states; France and China had joined the club. The USSR, the USA and the UK were the first to sign the NPT and 59 further nations quickly added their signatures. By 1975 the number had risen to about 80; it now stands at 115. Several countries, including India, have kept aloof, basically because they view the Treaty as one which has as its aim the prevention of other countries 'going nuclear'; that is to say, as a treaty which inhibits 'horizontal proliferation', but which does not impose any obligation on those countries that have already developed nuclear weapons to desist from the elaboration and growth of their own armouries in a process that has become called 'vertical proliferation'. Vertical proliferation implied the possibility of a USA/USSR hegemony that would determine the future of the world.

Since then India has exploded a nuclear device in an underground test, and speculation, both informed and uninformed, grows about the ability of certain other countries to take the same step. At least one country is believed to have stockpiled nuclear weapons without ever having carried out a test. There are, as I have said, no technical secrets about the way nuclear warheads are made. If a country has the scientific capacity and technological expertise together with the necessary industrial facilities, it would have no problem if it wanted to turn into a three-dimensional object the blueprints that would be provided by competent nuclear physicists and mathematicians. *What is highly significant is that there is no indication that any country's first nuclear device failed to explode: not the American, not the Soviet, not the British, not the French, not the Chinese; possibly not the Indian.*

It is not the least bit surprising that pressure 'to go nuclear' is exerted in some non-nuclear states by the military, by scientists and engineers, by journalists and by politicians. What else can be expected when the great powers proclaim that they are deploying hundreds or thousands of tactical nuclear weapons with their field armies? How can some of the smaller countries which are at war with each other be persuaded that these weapons are there to deter hostile action, that they are not a new form of artillery? The message conveyed by the fact that nuclear weapons were not used in the battles which saw the end of direct European influence in Indo-China, or in Korea and Vietnam or, in spite of the Foster Dulles doctrine of massive retaliation, to prevent the Soviet Union from suppressing the Hungarian revolt of 1956, totally fades in significance in contrast to the advertised possession of nuclear weapons by the great powers. Equally, the military value of nuclear weapons is regarded as having been proved when the Soviet Union, faced by the threat of a nuclear onslaught, withdrew from the situation that had been created when she started installing intermediate-range ballistic missiles (IRBMs) in Cuba. McGeorge Bundy, who was at

President Kennedy's right hand throughout the Cuban missile crisis, has written:[46]

'. . . the fact is that deterrence has worked, in all directions, since 1945. It is indeed a balance of terror . . . The one moment of relatively high danger, the Cuban Missile Crisis, proves the rule, for in that case no one on either side appears to have come close to giving, or recommending, an order for nuclear action; it was precisely because of their well justified fear of any such action that the main actors on both sides were so cautious. While occasional careless retrospective comments could suggest that nuclear decisions were near, the facts are opposite. Whatever the generals in various countries have said in support of their preferred systems or their asserted doctrines, both the words and the actions of civilian leaders . . . have shown a respectful awareness that *these weapons are different.*'

Nuclear weapons are clearly both the most powerful instruments of destruction and the most potent deterrent to aggression. Paradoxically, however, this has become one of the greatest dangers we face. The fact that the powers which already possess nuclear weapons have not used them in the 'hot' wars into which they have been drawn over the past two decades is no guarantee that they would not be used by poorly informed and less sophisticated countries. Once nuclear weapons were used anywhere, the battle could well involve the major powers in a nuclear holocaust. It would be cynical to agree with Mr. William C. Foster that in comparison with the United States and the Soviet Union some countries may have 'relatively little to lose if nuclear weapons are used'. But one can well agree with him[47] that 'having five nations with nuclear weapons is bad enough, and, if the number is to be limited, the prospects are almost certainly better at five than at six or any higher number.' As Helmut Schmidt has also put it,[40] 'The distribution of control over nuclear weapons among additional governments increases the probability of a nuclear catastrophe with mathematical certainty'.

The United Kingdom is a nuclear power because British nuclear scientists, helped by their refugee colleagues from Germany and Austria, were among those who first showed how the process of atomic fission could be exploited to make explosives of vastly greater force than their conventional chemical counterparts. The scientists who believed that providing more explosive power per unit of weight was a valuable military asset were not military men, nor did they sell the idea directly to the military. When Winston Churchill was told about the possibilities of atom bombs by Lord Cherwell (Professor Lindemann), his close friend and adviser, he is reported to have said[48] that he could not see any advantage in what was proposed; that chemical explosives were good enough for him.

The UK military chiefs were not asked for their views when in 1943 the decision was taken to combine the British with the American nuclear effort. It was not their affair. Nor were the military more than administrators in the American Manhattan Project, the code-name for the organisation that produced the first bombs, and in which British scientists became participants. Nor, again, did the military play a significant part in the debate that culminated in the dropping of the first atomic bombs on Hiroshima and Nagasaki. In this the American Air Force was executing a political decision. And as Clement Attlee, who in 1945 succeeded Churchill as Prime Minister, has related, the politicians knew nothing about nuclear weapons except that they were much more destructive than conventional bombs. As he wrote,[49] 'We knew nothing whatever at that time about the genetic effects of an atomic explosion. I knew nothing about fall-out and all the rest of what emerged after Hiroshima. As far as I know, President Truman and Winston Churchill knew nothing of these things either, nor did Sir John Anderson, who coordinated research on our side. Whether the scientists directly concerned knew, or guessed, I do not know. But if they did, then, so far as I am aware, they said nothing of it to those who had to make the decision.'

To the consternation of the British Government, cooperation with the Americans in nuclear technology (as opposed to basic nuclear research) broke down[50] in July 1946 with the passage of the McMahon Act, which decreed that the USA would no longer share nuclear secrets with any foreign country. Urged on by the wartime chief of the RAF, Lord Portal of Hungerford, who by then had moved to the Ministry of Supply as Controller of Atomic Energy, by the Chiefs of Staff, and by scientists and mathematicians who had participated in the Manhattan Project, Mr Attlee, the Prime Minister, and five members of his Cabinet — the others being kept in the dark — then decided to proceed independently to the development of a British bomb.[51] This highly secret decision, taken without any critical evaluation of the military advantages this step might confer, or of the repercussions of nuclear weaponry on foreign policy, automatically committed the whole government. The simple fact was that the United Kingdom was not prepared to allow the United States to be the one country that possessed a nuclear arsenal, any more than the Soviet Union was prepared to accept the Baruch Plan for the development of nuclear technology under United Nations control, a plan that was presented to the young United Nations by the Americans in June 1946. In the realisation that the USA would otherwise be the one power that might still continue to exploit 'the secret', the UK, like the USSR, decided to become an independent nuclear power. Since then the UK has remained 'independent', even if independence has necessitated American help. In fact the term 'independent' signifies little more than that the UK manufactures its own nuclear warheads, which at the start were designed as free-falling bombs to be carried by V-bombers. Today the nuclear warheads we produce are earmarked as weapons to be used in support of NATO operations, given that a 'theatre' war were ever to erupt in Europe.

When the age of missiles dawned in 1957, the UK embarked upon the development of a liquid-fuelled rocket called Blue Streak, which was essentially a copy of an early version of the American Atlas ballistic missile. This decision was a reaffirmation of the concept of independence. Given that we might have to face the Warsaw Pact powers alone, the declared policy of the United Kingdom from then on was that she would rely for security on an ability to strike Soviet targets with nuclear-armed ballistic missiles. National service came to an end not long after, and the country was informed that there could be no defence against nuclear attack.[25] Britain's shield from now on was to be the 'deterrent'. Politically the decision was enormously important.

The concept of Blue Streak was technically and operationally obsolete almost from the start, and in 1960 the project was abandoned. The United Kingdom then latched on to the American project to develop an air-launched ballistic missile, the one that went by the name of Skybolt. For a variety of reasons, mainly technological, the United States cancelled this project in 1962. The future of Britain's independent nuclear status suddenly became highly precarious. Under strong political pressure, the Americans then reluctantly agreed to the UK purchasing from them the submarine-launched Polaris missile, for which again the UK was to produce the nuclear warhead. But there were no military men at the 1962 Nassau Conference when Mr Macmillan persuaded President Kennedy to agree to the British request. The issue was essentially political. Now, according to a decision that has recently been agreed, Polaris will in due course be replaced by the MIRVed Trident missile, which in turn will assure the future of the UK's 'independent' nuclear status. Like the Polaris missile, the Trident will be purchased from the United States, but the nuclear warheads will be made in Britain.

A condition that applies to Polaris, and which will also apply to Trident, is that the UK's small submarine missile force of four boats is assigned to — which in practical terms means is targeted by — the NATO high command, with the proviso that, given a national emergency which in the view of the British Government calls for independent action, the Polaris (or Trident) boats could be withdrawn from the framework of NATO and used independently against, presumably, the USSR. There has never been any suggestion that the UK would ever be entitled to use American equipment against non-nuclear powers, or against one of our present Continental allies.

There are several aspects of the concept of British independence that should be noted. The first is that, having been an active participant at the start of the era of nuclear weapons, having become 'independent' in 1946 after the breakdown of cooperation with the Americans, the UK technically became a nuclear power on the day in 1952 that it exploded its first bomb. Sentiment is a powerful force in politics. The possession of nuclear weapons was regarded as a symbol of world power, and the UK was not going to abandon that status. This is the first point. The second is that the British nuclear arsenal is trivial in size in comparison with those of the USA and the USSR. The continued insistence on the status of 'independence' implies that the present British Government, like those before it, does not adhere to American or Soviet ideas about what constitutes nuclear sufficiency. It has given the seal of approval to the concept of 'minimal deterrence'; that is to say the British view is that the size of its nuclear force is adequate to deter aggression. There has never been any explicit statement to this effect, nor is there any clear indication that the British political and military leaders of today have reopened the discussions of the early sixties about the size of nuclear force necessary to maintain a state of mutual deterrence. The implicit British view of what constitutes a sufficient deterrent threat, as spelt out in 1980,[52] is, however, very important politically.

The third point is that while Harold Macmillan was impelled by political considerations in his struggle to persuade the Americans to sell us the Polaris missile in order to maintain the UK's 'independence', the successful outcome of his negotiations was nonetheless inconsistent with his even more determined fight to bring an end to the nuclear arms race. As one of his officials in both enterprises, the inconsistency did not strike me at the time. It does now, but because of the implication of 'independence' in relation to the concept of 'minimal deterrence', I am beginning to think that the undeclared and, to me then unrecognised, inconsistency may still prove of value.

A fourth question that needs to be asked is what is implied by the term 'national emergency', that is to say, in what circumstances would the United Kingdom initiate a nuclear exchange, with the Americans standing aside, knowing that, whatever national symbols might be painted on nuclear warheads before they were fired, they, and much else, would be unrecognisable after they had detonated? Would the targeting of a British warhead whose use was intended in the context of independence be in fact any different from what it would be in the framework of NATO?

France formally withdrew from the NATO Command structure because President de Gaulle was not prepared to delegate the defence of his country to the Americans. Nor was he ready to play second fiddle in negotiations with the

Soviet Union which then, as in the circumstances of the Nassau talks, posed the only real threat there was to the security of western Europe. The declared policy of France remains what it has always been since it became a nuclear power: to respond with nuclear weapons, come what may, to any intrusion of enemy forces on to French territory that could not be repelled with conventional arms. Whether this national strategic policy implies any greater realism than does that of the super-powers, or that of NATO, is highly dubious, but there is a technical difference. The independence of the United Kingdom is, at least in theory, conditional on American assent. That of France is not. On the other hand, the fact that French policy is also implicitly based on the concept of a minimal deterrent threat is important.

The fact that American military strength underpins the NATO alliance, and that America is committed to intervene in Europe's defence — if necessary with nuclear weapons — if Warsaw Pact forces were to invade NATO territory, has long been a matter of concern both for armchair strategists and for those who have represented the European powers in NATO councils. In the early sixties the State Department tried to persuade America's NATO allies to form a 'multilateral Polaris force'. The idea was that nationals of several NATO countries would man the same nuclear-armed submarines, the hope being that the existence of such a force would imply a sharing of responsibility if it ever came to the unleashing of nuclear war. It was also felt that by participating in such a force the sense of military inferiority and dependence felt by some of America's allies would be reduced.

In spite of much pressure from Washington, the idea failed, partly because of opposition emanating from American naval circles, and partly because of the lack of many, if indeed any, powerful advocates in Europe. The United

Kingdom was lukewarm to the idea. Participation in such a force would certainly have eroded the concept of British independence.

From time to time the idea of combining the British with the French nuclear forces has also been mooted. When, at the Nassau conference in 1962, America agreed to provide the United Kingdom with Polaris missiles, it was recognised that any such agreement would be regarded amiss by the French who, in consequence, might retaliate against the United Kingdom by continuing to block Britain's entry into the Common Market. It was for this reason that President Kennedy informed President de Gaulle of what was afoot, at the same time as he offered the French the same 'deal' which he was concluding with the British. The offer was rejected. Harold Wilson records in his memoirs[53] that when he became Prime Minister he reopened talks on nuclear matters with the French in an effort to achieve what he called 'a reverse Nassau'. Nothing came of the attempt to 'turn Nassau on to its head'. To the world at large, the United Kingdom and France are still pursuing independent nuclear courses.

This means that today there are four nuclear entities notionally and independently poised against the USSR from the west — the USA, NATO, the UK and France (there is China from the south). Whether this multiplicity of 'independent' nuclear threats faced by the Soviet Union increases or decreases the deterrent value of the nuclear armouries of the West is debatable. Obviously in a contest where those separately engaged have the same objective, namely that of winning, the outcome becomes more incalculable as the number of players increases beyond two. The incalculability that arises from there being three or four independent deterrent forces in the West may, therefore, increase the extent to which, because of uncertainty, the Soviet Union is deterred by Western strategic forces. On the other hand, if the Western deterrent forces were completely independent, there is no guarantee that the political objectives of the states to which they belong would always be the same. It is for this reason that some — for example, Helmut Schmidt — have argued that the solidarity of the Western alliance is weakened by the existence of separate nuclear forces.

Nonetheless, and in spite of certain possible short-term political gains which some believe would result from the reorganisation of the French, British, and perhaps part of the United States strategic nuclear forces into a 'NATO strategic deterrent', it is difficult to see what would be the military advantage. A NATO strategic nuclear force could no more hold up an all-out Soviet conventional attack than would the present threat that NATO would in such circumstances resort to the use of the theatre and tactical nuclear weapons that are drawn from the arsenals of the USA and the UK. Moreover, to make military sense, a NATO strategic force would have to be under single command. Until real political unity, as yet not within sight, develops both within Europe and between a cohesive Europe and the USA, it would be pointless to embark upon the organisation of a separate NATO nuclear force, even though Europe cannot count on the USA necessarily risking its own destruction were the Soviet Union, for whatever reason, to make an aggressive move against the Western alliance.

If anything should be a spur towards the goal of real European unity, surely this should be.

CHAPTER 6

The Arms Race

Effective military power implies an ability to bring force to bear in order to inhibit an enemy from doing something which is held to be hostile to one's interests, or to defeat him if he embarks on such action. In war, force is applied to stop one's adversary, if needs be by crushing him in the field; and if that cannot be done in a precise way, it has become military doctrine that everything around him should be destroyed in an effort to stop him. Over the years this has meant a transition from hand-to-hand fighting to an ability to fire ballistic missiles, armed with nuclear warheads, over thousands of miles with an accuracy relatively greater than that which any expert marksman could ever hope to achieve on a rifle-range, and with the capacity of destroying utterly, and with a single blow, enormous cities thousands of miles away.

From the mid-thirties onwards, there has been an unceasing technological race between the great powers in every field of armaments, in the effort to increase the range, speed, accuracy and payload of aircraft; in developing a variegated family of missiles; in improving the fire-power, armour, speed and manoeuvrability of tanks; in improving small arms; in developing night-sighting techniques; and in exploiting radar and laser technology. Given that it had the endurance, a few years ago it would have taken the fastest military aircraft, less than, say, ten hours to fly from the mid-West of America to Moscow. Today a Minuteman ballistic missile can travel the distance in thirty minutes, and be no less certain of finding its target. Theoretically, the technological achievement which the Polaris concept implies is even more astonishing, for here the missile is launched onto its ballistic path, not from a fixed point on land, but from any one of an infinity of points under the waters. The navigational equipment of the submarine, aided by space satellite beacons, is so precise that at the moment of launch the computing system involved will have fed into it figures that give the coordinates of the starting point of the flight path of the missile. Computers instantaneously do the rest of the calculations, which determine such things as the rate at which the solid fuel motors of the missile burn, and the varying positions of the jets necessary to put and keep the missile on its selected ballistic path. All this has come about through vast improvements in liquid and solid fuel technology; through enormous advances in inertial navigational techniques based on what were once simple gyroscopes; through the elaboration of electronic servo-mechanism devices and accelerometers; and through highly advanced radio and radar techniques. The 'manoeuvrable bus' of a MIRVed missile has considerably extended these techniques. To many people, the most spectacular result of all this applied science has no doubt been manned artificial satellites orbiting the earth. To others, an even greater technical achievement was the photographing of the back of the moon over 240,000 miles away, and more recently, of the surface of Mars and Saturn's rings. The flight path to Mars was some 400 million miles; to Saturn, three times as far. As I have said, the advances in aeronautics of recent years, including the development of supersonic jet aircraft, of vertical take-off aircraft, and of variable geometry aircraft, hardly compare in their strategic significance with those that have been made in rocket technology. But aircraft and rockets constitute only one facet of the process whereby force is now brought to bear in the exercise of military power. The massing and speeding of movements of men have been much improved, as have communications and the gathering and dissemination of intelligence. Whether much of this has affected the outcome of the scores of wars that have disturbed the peace these past thirty years is another matter.

The pace of the arms race has probably been faster since the end of the Second World War than it has ever been in all human history. So too has its scale and cost. In the United States expenditure on research and development has accounted over the years for a steady 11 percent of the total defence budget (and about half of the Federal funds that go to all R and D). It is expected to remain at the same level now that projected outlays on defence are being planned to exceed $200 billion. In his valedictory Statement to Congress,[54] Dr William Perry, who served as Under Secretary for Defense Research and Engineering during President Carter's administration, urged that it should, basing himself on the proposition that over the past ten years Soviet investment in military research equipment and building has increased annually at a steady 4 per cent, and that the Americans must therefore 'catch up'. The manner of calculation leading to this conclusion is not very convincing, but Dr Perry concluded his message in terms that were calculated to strike fear in the hearts and minds of Senators and Congressmen.

Measured in terms of 1972 constant dollars, US military R and D in 1960 cost 11 billion dollars. This figure was more than double the 1953 figure. By 1980 it had risen to $13.5 billion, ten times more than the sum allocated to defence R and D in the United Kingdom, which nonetheless consumes more than half (55 per cent) of the total of government funds that go to all R and D. In France the corresponding figure is 33 per cent, and in West Germany 12 per cent. In absolute terms the United Kingdom spends more on military R and D than any other European country. What the USSR spends on military R and D is not known. F. A. Long (for many years associated officially with American defence policy and who with J. Reppy edited *The Genesis of New Weapons*[55]) recently wrote[56] that 'on the criteria which the US military have advanced for their programmes, emphasis on advanced technology and first development of innovative weapons, the USSR record does not seem very impressive. For a large majority of the currently important weapons, first introduction has come from the US or other western nations, with the USSR typically in the follow-on role. If this is a valid analysis, the current US alarm about the large USSR programme of military R & D seems disingenuous and, for the military at least, self-serving.'

The enormous volume of resources that is now devoted to military R and D is a function not only of the scale of the effort, but also of the rising cost of the increasingly complex technological devices that it is hoped to incorporate in new armaments. Increasing complexity imposes its penalties. One immediate consequence is that the cost of the R and D which goes into the making of any major item of modern military equipment can be enormous, and is frequently so great in relation to the likely sums that would be demanded for production that the project has to be abandoned before completion. The British TSR 2 aircraft project, when it was cancelled early in 1965, had already consumed £125 million in R and D[57]. At the time, this was equivalent to the total sum spent annually on recurrent expenditure in all British universities. Skybolt, the air-launched nuclear ballistic missile, had cost $500 million in R and D before it was cancelled in 1962 by the American Government[58]. Mauler, an American anti-aircraft missile, was dropped at about the same time after $200 million had been spent on its development[59].

One of the reasons why projects such as these go on being cancelled is that the resources their development demand are clearly excessive in relation to the military needs which they are designed to satisfy. Sometimes the 'needs' have evaporated before the project is well on the way. 'If it works, it's obsolete', is the cynical comment of many a member of a military R and D establishment. Often, too, it becomes clear as development proceeds that certain technical problems which it had been assumed at the start could be overcome are far too difficult to solve. Clearly, too, the longer it takes to complete a project, the more costly it becomes. The American space shuttle took three years longer than planned to reach its flying trials. This entailed a cost of nearly $11 billion, 60 per cent more than was envisaged at the start, an 'overrun' equivalent to some 25 per cent of the whole British defence budget. If it goes ahead, the American MX ballistic missile system, costed at $30 billion, will consume, it is estimated, at least $50 billion. It is already rumoured that the British Trident programme which was announced only last year, and on which, apart from the warheads, little significant work can have been started as yet, will cost at least 10 per cent more than estimated. In the UK the development costs of advanced technological projects that are taken to completion in numbers sufficient to satisfy our own requirements are usually a very significant proportion of the whole cost of producing the new weapon. The Tornado, the advanced multi-role military aircraft that is being produced jointly by the UK, West Germany and Italy, has cost many times more than was estimated when the decision was taken to embark on the project, the programme now consuming 6 to 7 per cent of the UK's defence budget[60]. It is reported that each aircraft will now cost the Germans 75 million marks, nearly three times as much as was estimated in 1973 (an interval over which inflation averaged only about five per cent a year), and seven times the figure estimated in 1964. As has been pointed out[61], 'by 1984 the Tornado project looks like swallowing up more than a quarter of Germany's defence equipment budget'.

Forty years ago, that is to say during the Second World War, the arms race was still to a large extent a race for quantity, even though in some cases radical qualitative improvements, e.g. in naval fire control equipment, had a great impact on operations. In recent decades the arms race has been a race for quality, at whatever point the race has been entered, even though equipment that is most advanced technically has not necessarily proved to be the most useful in the wars in which nations have been engaged over the past two decades. High technology certainly did not pay off in Vietnam.

In the Lees Knowles Lectures which I delivered in Cambridge in 1965, and which were later published[62], I spelt out some general lessons that could then be derived from the apparent consequences of the arms race. Little attention was paid at the time to what I had to say, but as current (1981) debates on British defence policy make only too clear, the lessons as I saw them then remain relevant The first is that efforts to incorporate into new weapon systems technical knowledge that has not yet been established or perfected inevitably proves very expensive and often fails. A second is that, with few exceptions, each new generation within classes of equipment costs much more per unit weapon than the one it replaces. I illustrated this lesson with examples of the period. More recently published figures show that one American F.15 fighter plane today costs about $20 million, a single XM-1 tank $1 million, and one round of ammunition for a standard anti-tank gun $5,000. The increase varies in scale between different types of equipment, but even when one makes full allowance for the effects of inflation, one cannot find any examples, except possibly very standard items such as small-arms ammunition, where the application of more science and technology has led to a reduction in the cost of individual weapons[63]. The cost of naval vessels and other equipment in which the heavy engineering industry is involved about doubles between successive generations. The incoming generation of British medium bombers in the early 1960s was some ten times more expensive than its pre-war counterpart. Today, the Chieftain tank costs twice as much as the Centurion; the Seawolf guided weapon costs seven times as much as the Seacat; a Jaguar aircraft costs three times what a Hunter 60 cost; and a Tornado, for which the most recent figure is £14.3 million, forty times what a Spitfire of the Second World War cost.

I then pointed out a third consequence of the technological arms race; that each new generation of equipment makes greater demands than its predecessor for skilled supporting personnel. The situation has since worsened. A study[64] carried out in the United States indicates that in spite of the fact that the US Air Force has invested $52 billion on fighter planes in recent years, the result has been a fall in their numbers and their readiness. About half of America's fleet of F.15 fighter planes is said to be unserviceable at any one time; about 70 per cent of the F.III D aircraft, and about a third of the A.10s. Moreover, since the start of the sixties, the need for technically qualified maintenance personnel has gone up 40 per cent. It is true that the aim is generally to put into the hands of front-line soldiers equipment which is more certain in its operation and which calls for less maintenance at that level. But if this aim is realised, the problem of skilled manpower is not solved. As always, it is merely shifted to another level. Rationally it does not matter whether this level is military or civilian; the trained men have to be found somewhere.

Because of the increasing complexity and cost of weapons,

there is a trend which I likened to an 'inexorable law' that affects the cost of defence R and D, and a term on which Harold Wilson, when Prime Minister, set a seal of approval in a speech to Parliament in 1964[65]. If, as I put it, 'a country wishes its forces to live up to the standards set by the arms race between the super-powers, it needs to re-equip them at frequent intervals with weapons that are more sophisticated, and therefore much more expensive, than previous equipment. At this point considerations of the absolute size of the economy come into play. The cost of developing a weapon system of a given degree of sophistication is much the same in all advanced industrialised countries. But the greater the 'buy' over which the costs can be spread, the lower the resultant unit cost. For this reason alone, the United States and the Soviet Union by their very size can always expect to produce sophisticated weapon systems more cheaply than we can in Britain.'

Let us suppose that the Gross National Product of the United Kingdom were to rise as a result of the greater productivity of what is a more or less static working population — which it is hardly doing now — and that the same proportion each year were devoted to defence. 'Would we be able', I asked, 'to "buy more defence" because of the greater absolute amount of money that would be going to the armed forces?' (I was talking in terms of money values standardised to take account of the effects of inflation.) The answer is No. New aircraft, new surface-to-air missiles, new radars, cost more than their predecessors. At the same time, improvements in the sophistication or effectiveness of our own weapon systems tend to be cancelled out by those that are introduced by our potential enemy who, in his efforts to counter our own more expensive offensive systems spends even more resources in trying to devise new technological defences. The net result is an increase in expenditure on defence equipment by both parties, and usually an increase in the security of neither.

But on the other hand, if one side or the other unilaterally curtailed its defence expenditure, it would soon find itself at a military disadvantage. This is the fear that lies behind the arms race. The pace of the race is not determined by the UK; it is set by the two super-powers.

Over the past five years, between 42 and 47 per cent of the UK's annual defence budget has been consumed by pay, pensions, housing, feeding and clothing. The other half, according to the published official 1981 Defence Review, has gone on building of one sort or another, for example, on barracks and airfields; on the purchase of weapons, including aircraft and ships; and on research and development. But as fast as the GNP has risen, so there has been a corresponding rise in the cost of providing for the men the Services need. Only to a small extent do the armed services consume goods whose relative costs would decrease as a result of increases in productivity in the industries concerned. 'If one were to assume that the proportion of the Gross National Product that goes to defence were to remain constant, it would mean that, *at best*, no more than the same proportion of the defence budget would be available each year for procurement and research.' This conclusion is as true today as it was twenty years ago.

But 'the best' has not happened. The GNP of the UK today, standing at something like £190 billion, is about 60 per cent higher than it was 20 years ago. But the proportion that has gone to defence has fallen from a level of 6.5 per cent in the financial year 1960-61 to 5 per cent today. In standardised money terms the defence estimates have in fact decreased over the period from the level of £10.3 thousand million to £9.6 thousand million. The consequences are only what could have been expected. Since the overall cost of keeping a uniformed man in the field has on average risen from £18,500 twenty years ago to not far from £30,000 today, the number of uniformed men, excluding reserves, has fallen from 559,000 in 1960 to 329,000. This was only to have been expected. Even if we had been prepared to spend an increasing proportion of our GNP on defence, we could have afforded to re-equip them with technologically much more advanced and vastly more costly weapon systems only if we had accepted forces which had diminished in number more than they have (diminished in uniformed manpower, that is; not necessarily in fire-power).

While the consequences of increasing sophistication are inescapable, they can to some extent be abated. For example, we could choose weapons that are being produced in greater quantity than the ones they replace. In practice, however, this would mean a smaller variety of equipment, and since modern weapons are usually specialised for different roles, we would then be forced to abandon some of our military commitments. Another measure which could mitigate would be to lessen the load of research and development costs by buying weapons from countries that are producing them in quantity. But neither of these measures would prove to be more than a palliative. Even with larger scale production, new equipment tends to be much more expensive than that which precedes it. (Indeed, it is so expensive that without much more successful standardisation with our allies than has been achieved so far, it is bound to be ordered in smaller quantities than before.)

The consequences of the technological arms race, that is of the 'inexorable law' of R and D to which we have been subjected since the end of the Second World War, may not have been consciously planned, but they were nonetheless inevitable. In theory the UK has been forced to choose between altering its tasks so as to avoid the need to introduce some of the most expensive weapon systems, or of making its forces smaller. In fact the UK has been driven to a combination of both measures. The United Kingdom has had to reduce its commitments worldwide. It has withdrawn from the Far East, from the Gulf, from the Middle East. And it is still overstretched. As Mr Nott, the Secretary of State for Defence, stated in a parliamentary debate on 19th May, 1981[66], 'We have a choice. Either we can continue to pretend that there is no problem, that we can wish away the threat or imagine that the United Kingdom can somehow sustain, replace and enhance its operational effectiveness without a fresh look at how we perform our tasks — what we are doing, and why — or we can continue to drift down the path that led, this year and last to cuts in ammunition, fuel, training and deployment, and will lead inevitably in the next few years to increasingly degraded operational ability.'

In his valedictory report to Congress[54], Dr Perry recognised that the increasing technical sophistication in weapons systems imposes a heavy penalty in rising costs, both for the Americans and for the Russians. But he does not appear to realise the other penalties, above all that even today's richest countries will be driven by the arms race down the same road of decreasing power — as I pointed out when I first formulated the 'inexorable law of R and D'. The same conclusion is now spelt out by James Fallows, the author of a valuable work on national defence in the USA[67], in a penetrating review[68] of four books which discuss current American defence problems. The United States, he writes, often has to face the choice between the complex and the simple path when deciding about new weapon systems. 'The complex alternatives emphasize rarefied technical developments — powerful radar and computer systems in aircraft, sophisticated sensors in guided missiles, high-acceleration engines in tanks — which are inherently more expensive and less reliable than simpler systems.' The Pentagon, he goes on to say, 'often chooses needlessly complex systems that leave it with a smaller force than expected', with 'fewer weapons in the field', and with less money to maintain them, 'train crews or stock spare parts'. 'The military is left', as he puts it, 'with a force that few would have chosen had they allowed for unforeseen consequences.'

In short, the arms race can bankrupt the super-powers without adding anything to their respective military strengths. Deterrent systems today cost tens of times more than they did twenty years ago, when the political state of deterrence was just as operative as it is today. From the point of view of political/strategic value, nothing has been gained.

In view of the enormously far-reaching but unwanted political and economic consequences of the technological arms race, consequences which do not accord with the assumed aims of the race, it is all but impossible to believe that the process of defence R and D is under rational control. Ideal systems can be set out on paper whereby operational requirements are first defined in relation to clear military needs, and then translated into technological projects which are formulated against the background of all available scientific knowledge.[69] In some countries, and certainly in the USA, military men who have specialised in engineering, and some who are also well-informed about scientific matters, cooperate closely with civilian scientists and engineers in the R and D and procurement processes. In the United States there is a well-known organisation which goes by the acronym ARPA (Advanced Research Projects Agency) which was launched in 1957 under the direction of Herbert York, the first head of Defense Research and Engineering in the Pentagon. This Agency is still in being, with a staff consisting of a majority of civilian scientists and engineers, aided by selected military men.

Theory and practice in military R and D are, however, remote from each other. Numbers of major and very costly projects have been started in the United States and then, for one or another reason, cancelled before completion; for example, redundancy, the escalation of costs, or because the system simply did not work. I doubt indeed if military R and D is any more effectively controlled in the United States than it is in the United Kingdom, where the formal machinery to define operational requirements and to control projects goes on being 'reformed' year after year in the light of bitter experience.

As Chief Scientific Adviser to the Minister of Defence in the years 1960 to 1966, I tried to coordinate the UK's smaller defence R and D effort with the much bigger one of the USA. First Herbert York, and then his successor Harold Brown, agreed seemingly foolproof ways whereby we in the United Kingdom could avoid wasting resources through unnecessary duplication of American work, and whereby the United States would benefit from British work. Nothing came of our efforts. It turned out that every project that might have been moved to one or other side of the Atlantic already had a competitor which could not be abandoned because so much had already been committed to it both by industry and by its supporters in the Services, whether navy, army or air force. If the UK had developed a ground-to-air missile of promise, so had the USA. If a new tank, its competitor was always there. In his final statement to Congress, Dr Perry observed[54] that this situation had improved somewhat during the course of his four-year reign. One can only hope that he is not over-optimistic. If the process of military R and D and procurement were as well organised as corresponding activities in some parts of civil manufacturing industry, the efforts of the past thirty years to standardise NATO's arms would not have proved as unrewarding as they have — and the arms trade not as competitive as it is!

It is my view, derived from many years of experience, that the basic reason for the irrationality of the whole process is the fact that ideas for a new weapon system derive in the first place, not from the military, but from different groups of scientists and technologists who are concerned to replace or improve old weapons systems — for example, by miniaturising components — or by reducing weight/yield ratios of nuclear warheads so that they can be carried further by a ballistic missile (that is to say, by packing greater explosive power into a smaller volume and weight). At base, the momentum of the arms race is undoubtedly fuelled by the technicians in governmental laboratories and in the industries which produce the armaments.

Sadly, there is nothing new in this. It has always been so. Indeed history has never been ashamed to name the heroes of the arms race. For example, while Archimedes is renowned for his preoccupation with mathematical research and, like Plato, is said to have held mechanical contrivances derived from the exploitation of pure science in low regard, he nonetheless also designed fortifications and many engines of war, including a great catapult, in order to help Hiero keep at bay the Romans who were besieging Syracuse in the latter part of the third century BC. Leonardo da Vinci, whose genius lives in his paintings and drawings, was equally one of the great scientists, and probably the greatest mechanical engineer and military scientist of his day. The letter which he wrote to Ludovico Sforza, the ruler of the principality of Milan, offering to provide any instruments of war which he could desire — military bridges, mortars, mines, chariots, catapults, and 'other machines of marvellous efficacy not in common use' — was that of an arms salesman, the sort of offer which a later generation might have regarded as emanating from a 'merchant of death'. Michelangelo, whom we know as the greatest sculptor of the Renaissance and the painter of the frescoes in the Sistine Chapel, was at one moment in his career engineer-in-chief of the fortifications of Florence. No contemporary Englishman was as versatile, but the profession of armourer has always been held in high regard. The office of Master of the King's Ordnance, later to be Master-General, was established as early as 1414, with his workshop in the Tower of London where under his direction the King's artificers followed their skilled trades. It was here that guns were made, using all the metallurgical knowledge of the day, in the first half of the fifteenth century. This was the start of the British Ordnance Board which continues to this day, although with a different postal address. And the Master-General still goes on, although he is no longer President of the Board. Nor does he enjoy, as he did until 1828, the honour of a seat in the Cabinet.

The emerging scientists and engineers of the Renaissance were, of course, involved with far more than just armour and fire-arms. Stimulated by what they perceived to be other needs of their political and military masters, craftsmen and scholars busied themselves with devices to aid navigation, and with signalling systems like the heliograph and the semaphore. Those who followed their example during and after the period of the Second World War were behaving in precisely the same way, anticipating needs long before they were recognised by those who would use whatever was invented. So it was that Whittle, an engineer and Royal Air Force officer, designed the jet engine; that Randall and Boot, working in Oliphant's department in Birmingham, invented the cavity magnetron, an instrument which transformed radar and which has been described[70] as 'the key to the destruction of Germany from the air'; that Draper of MIT elaborated gyroscopes into the inertial guidance systems without which neither modern aviation nor space technology would be what they are; that the best brains in the field of nuclear physics — Oppenheimer, Peierls, Fermi, Szilard, to mention only a few — showed how the process of fission could be harnessed to make 'The Bomb'. These men, and numbers of others who were working at the frontiers of scientific and engineering knowledge, produced new devices when it was barely possible to perceive their relation to the military operations that were then in progress.

This process applies not only to nuclear projects. What is now the successful British aircraft, the Harrier, began life on the drawing board, went through its prototype development and into production, in the face of the opposition of the Royal Air Force. It was entirely a French, American and British civilian conception, stimulated in the first instance by the American Mutual Weapons Development Project team. Only after it had proved itself did the British services and then the American Marine Air Force take it up.

In the nuclear world of today, military chiefs, who by convention are a country's official advisers on national security, as a rule merely serve as the channel through which the men in the laboratories transmit their views. For it is the man in the laboratory, not the soldier or sailor or airman, who at the start proposes that for this or that reason it would be useful to improve an old or devise a new nuclear warhead; and if a new warhead, then a new missile; and, given a new missile, a new system within which it has to fit. It is he, the technician, not the commander in the field, who starts the process of formulating the so-called military need. It is he who has succeeded over the years in equating, and so confusing, nuclear destructive power with military strength, as though the former were the single and a sufficient condition of military success. The men in the nuclear weapons laboratories of both sides have succeeded in creating a world with an irrational foundation, on which a new set of political realities has in turn had to be built. They have become the alchemists of our times, working in secret ways that cannot be divulged, casting spells which embrace us all. They may never have been in battle, they may never have experienced the devastation of war; but they know how to devise the means of destruction. And the more destructive power there is, so, one must assume they imagine, the greater the chance of military success.

Recent decisions on nuclear matters illustrate this quite plainly. Two years ago it was announced that the British Polaris warheads had been rebuilt to incorporate not only the nuclear explosive but also decoys. It is now public knowledge,[71] however, that the men in the British nuclear weapons laboratory had set to work on the project, called Chevaline, as far back as the late sixties, without at the start seeking ministerial or any other approval. Presumably only their representatives in the Ministry of Defence then knew what they were doing: designing decoys for the Polaris missiles in order to confuse a barely existent Soviet ABM system. Their opposite numbers in the American weapons laboratories had worked on the same devices until the operational futility of ABM systems was formally admitted by both the USA and the USSR at the SALT I talks. As McGeorge Bundy has put it,[20] 'The ABM Treaty [of 1972] made a virtue of what most experts thought a technological necessity'. But the British Government was not party to the SALT talks, and Chevaline was not halted when the Americans and Russians agreed not to deploy ABM defences; nor, one must imagine, was the functional uselessness of Chevaline — now admitted to have cost £1000 million — explained to any effect to the British Cabinet, even though David Owen, who in 1978 became Foreign Secretary in James Callaghan's Government, and who was committed to the achievment of meaningful agreements in the field of disarmament, had pointed out in a book which he published in 1972,[72] two years after he ceased being a junior minister in charge of the Royal Navy, that the system was technically unnecessary. He has also since disclosed[73] that shortly after it again assumed power in 1974, the Labour Government could have taken the decision to cancel the Chevaline programme when the matter was discussed at a Cabinet meeting on November 20, 1974, and that by 1977 and 1978, by when 'most of the Chevaline money had been spent or was already contracted for ... the only credible arguments for continuing were the political not military aspects of our [UK] deterrence strategy'.

Had the Russians made operational what was only the partially effective and limited ABM system which they had been building to protect Moscow, it would have been the only one in the country. Strategically it would have mattered not one whit if, given a nuclear war, the relatively few British Polaris missiles had been aimed, not at Moscow, but at any one of hundreds of Soviet strategic targets which were clearly undefended. Regardless of what research into ABM systems still goes on in both the USA and the USSR, and of what success it might achieve, if any, the situation so far as the United Kingdom is concerned remains the same.

It has also been revealed[74] that before any decison had been taken by the British Government to replace Polaris with Trident, long before the need for any such decision had been put to Ministers, the men in the British nuclear weapons laboratory had pre-empted the situation. They had not only started to design a warhead for a MIRVed Trident missile; they had also, with American help, conducted underground tests of their designs. Presumably there were a few in the British military establishment who knew and understood what was afoot.

A more important current illustration of the way men in the R and D laboratories pre-empt strategic decisions — and therefore add rigidity to political discussion — is the cruise missile. This weapon came into being, as Dr Perry explained in his Statement[54] to Congress, as one of four major projects designed to modernise the American strategic nuclear forces, in particular because, being a 'stand-off' weapon, it imparted 'survivability' to the B.52 bombers which otherwise might become vulnerable to Soviet air defences. 'Fullscale development' of the cruise missile began in 1977, the implication being that R and D to produce such a weapon system began several years earlier. The proposed land-based missile is thus a development of a system whose genesis is to be found in the effort to improve the chances that the B.52 strategic bomber would survive given that it was ever used to launch nuclear warheads on to Soviet territory. The political reaction in certain NATO countries to the suggested deployment of these weapons on their territory was clearly not anticipated.

There lies the problem. The nuclear world of today has come about because basic scientific enquiries into the nature of matter led to an understanding of atomic structure, and so to the demonstration that the atom could be split with the release of vast amounts of energy. From that moment technology assumed command. A new future with its anxieties was shaped by technologists, not because they were concerned with any visionary picture of how the world should evolve, but because they were merely doing what they saw to be their job.

CHAPTER 7

The Advice of Scientists

No one knows what Franklin D. Roosevelt, the American President, or Winston Churchill, the British Prime Minister, appreciated in 1945 about the significance of the atom bomb to the world's future. Attlee's record implies they understood very little. To most of the scientists who were concerned in its development, the atom bomb at the start was merely something that had enormously more destructive power than chemical explosives. But a few nuclear scientists, Nils Bohr in particular, did understand that, given an atom bomb, the world would never again be the same. When Fermi demonstrated in 1942 with the help of his experimental 'pile' that the atoms of a particular isotope of uranium could be split (by the bombardment of Uranium 235 with sub-atomic neutron particles), they realised that the atom could either be used in controlled fashion to produce theoretically limitless electric power, or in a different way to release virtually unbounded destructive force. The worst fears of these far-seeing scientists were realised when the first 'bomb' was successfully detonated in the deserts of New Mexico on July 16, 1945. Other physicists then joined Bohr in trying to make those in authority understand that what had happened was not just a quantitative change in the power to destroy, but a qualitative leap infinitely more far-reaching than the discovery of gunpowder itself. Hiroshima and Nagasaki nonetheless followed.

There is no indication that any of the Soviet leaders of the day had any doubts about the wisdom of proceeding to the development of nuclear weapons. There was certainly no public debate. Indeed, as is now known, the Soviet nuclear programme had merely been interrupted when the German armies poured eastwards until they were halted outside Moscow, on a line stretching from Leningrad in the north to Stalingrad in the south. As soon as it could be, the programme was resumed in the most vigorous way possible.

In the United States, however, the debate about nuclear weapons became vocal after the war. Encouraged by eager but uncomprehending politicians and military men, those scientists who wanted to press on with the development of bombs were on one side of the barricades. Those who questioned the military and social consequences of what had been achieved were on the other. The story, with its dramatic climax in 1954 in the public humiliation of Oppenheimer, the man who had directed the making of the first bomb, is too well-known to need retelling. Those who sided with him, and who wanted to see the growth of nuclear armouries halted, were all but branded as enemies of the state. It was an attitude that was not peculiar to the United States. An anonymous piece of ironic doggerel which circulated in official circles in London in the early sixties epitomised the clash of attitudes:

'Breathes there the man with soul so dead.
Or so peculiar in the head
So treacherous to his native land,
He thinks the H-bomb should be banned,
Or that defenders of the West,
Should store the bomb without a test?
Who on his side in witness calls
Superfluous sermons from St Paul's,
Or Dr Schweitzer, or the Pope,
Or pseudo-scientific dope,

When mighty minds that rule the State
The great deterrent vindicate
(All good and honourable men,
Pinning their faith on hydrogen)
Maintaining Britain's place and pride
With armament of genocide?'

One or two of the British scientists who had participated in the Manhattan Project remained in the States. Others formed the nucleus of the British team which, starting at Harwell, set about the task of providing the United Kingdom with its own bomb. There was no public discussion as in America. At the start Parliament was completely in the dark.[51] Only a very few in the higher echelons of the military knew. It is on record[75] that Sir Henry Tizard, who soon after the war left Oxford to return to London as chairman of two new governmental bodies, the Advisory Council on Scientific Policy (the ACSP) and the Defence Research Policy Committee (the DRPC), vainly advised against what was being proposed. Although two other members of the ACSP must certainly have been in the picture, I, its Deputy Chairman, knew nothing of what was going on. The scientist who spoke out publicly in the United Kingdom against the development of nuclear weapons was Patrick Blackett, later, as Lord Blackett, to become President of the Royal Society. But Blackett was regarded as a 'red', and few listened to the arguments he set out in his book, *Military and Political Consequences of Atomic Energy*;[76] which was published in 1948, the year before the Russians revealed to the world that they too knew how to make an atomic bomb.

Blackett's opposition to all 'strategic' bombing, and to almost anything — including the bomb — which Lord Cherwell favoured, was coloured by much prejudice, and the book makes strange reading today. Some of the arguments are dubious, but the thrust of the volume was right. Blackett was seeing clearly into the future when he wrote that: 'The dropping of the atomic bombs was not so much the last military act of the second world war, as the first act of a cold diplomatic war with Russia.' In support of his view that the possession by the USA of nuclear weapons would drive the USSR 'to ensure by all possible means that her effective military frontiers are pushed as far away from the Russian homeland as possible', he cited a statement made in 1946 by Henry Wallace, formerly Vice President to Franklin D. Roosevelt:

'There is a school of military thinking which recognizes these facts, recognizes that when several nations have atomic bombs, a war which will destroy modern civilization will result and that no nation can win such a war. This school of thought therefore advocates a "preventative war", an attack on Russia now before Russia has atomic bombs. This scheme is not only immoral but stupid. If we should attempt to destroy all the principal Russian cities and her heavy industry, we might well succeed. But the immediate counter-measure which such an attack would call for is the prompt occupation of all continental Europe by the Red Army. Would we be prepared to destroy the cities of all Europe in trying to finish what we started? The idea is so contrary to all the basic instincts and principles of the American people that any such action would be possible only under a dictatorship at home.'

In France, recovering from the war, the position was much the same as in the United Kindom. French scientists who had played a highly significant part, first in the Anglo-French and then in the Anglo-French-Canadian nuclear effort, felt bitter when they found themselves left out in the cold not only by the Americans but also by the British.[77] They then set to work in order to provide France with a nuclear capability, at first secretly but with all secrecy about what they were doing vanishing when General de Gaulle became President in 1958.

The nuclear debate in the USA became muted for a short time after Oppenheimer had been deprived of his 'clearances' at the time of the public enquiry that had been stimulated by his opposition to the development of the H-bomb. Disquiet about the deleterious effects of radioactive fallout resulting from the testing of nuclear weapons then began to spread all over the world. The words Strontium 90 and Iodine 131 started to be bandied about in the papers. There had been the disastrous incident of the Japanese fishermen who were caught in the fallout from the Bikini series of H-bomb tests in 1954. The fallout from one 15-megaton shot in this series of tests covered an area of 7,000 square miles. Information about the continuing damaging effects of radiation on those who had survived the Hiroshima and Nagasaki explosions became common knowledge. A powerful and world-wide Campaign for Nuclear Disarmament (CND) sprang into being. Calls for an end to the testing of nuclear weapons were heard everywhere, even in the USSR, where in 1959 a number of scientists were allowed to express their disquiet. Among those who raised their voices, presumably with the approval of the authorities, was Andrei Sakharov. Before this his name was unknown in the West. Earlier, in 1956, Adlai Stevenson had made the suspension of tests a major issue in his unsuccessful campaign to win the US presidential election. It was inevitable that something had to be done.

Formal diplomatic and technical talks were started in Geneva to consider an international agreement to ban all tests. Scientists from various countries, accompanied by representatives of their respective political authorities, gathered to discuss the problem. From the moment that the meetings of 'experts' started, it was evident, however, that there was not going to be much agreement. Politicians, including at first Eisenhower, wanted a comprehensive test ban. Preying on and exacerbating suspicions of cheating, but driven essentially by the wish to continue the development of nuclear weapons — with little, if indeed any, appreciation of their actual military as opposed to their deterrent value — the weapons experts of both sides, aided and abetted by their willing military colleagues, saw to it that if a ban on testing were to be agreed politically, it should not be one that precluded testing underground, where there was no danger of radioactive contamination affecting people, animals, or vegetation. A moratorium on any testing had, in fact, been agreed by Eisenhower and Khrushchev. It lasted from 1958 to 1961, but was openly campaigned against by even the head of the American Atomic Energy Commission, who was not averse to seeking support for his views in the UK. It was not surprising that the moratorium was broken by the Russians after President Eisenhower had declared that the Americans felt free to resume testing, but would give advance notice, and after the Russians had indicated that they were disturbed by the continuation of testing by the French.[78]

The Oppenheimer affair had polarised a prominent part of the American scientific community. Some who until then had been unquestioning in the help they had given the Defense Department started to voice their doubts in public debate. They began to ask whether the arms race, and in particular the nuclear arms race, was enhancing or detracting from America's security. They began to question the need for further tests.

In comparison with what took place in the United States, there was no sophisticated public debate about the test ban in the United Kingdom. This was partly because there is a bigger gulf between academic and defence scientists and engineers in the UK than exists in the USA. Partly, too, it was because matters which in the USA can be read about in the open literature, such as Congressional records, are often treated as 'secret' in the UK; partly, also, because British scientists were in general uninterested. At the start I, too, was uninterested. But from the moment I was appointed Chief Scientific Adviser to the Minister of Defence, I became infected by Harold Macmillan's commitment to a cessation of all nuclear tests. The studies which I had made had led to the clear conclusion that, while nuclear weapons deter, they are not weapons with which to fight wars. A state of mutual deterrence was clearly operating by the end of the fifties. I could see no point in further testing nor, as I have said, did I see any inconsistency between the aim of stopping the nuclear arms race on the one hand, and the United Kingdom assuring its 'independent' status as a nuclear power on the other.

The nuclear arms race had been in progress all but fifteen years before senior scientific advisers to the governments concerned first tried to put on the brakes. Overtly, the race had started in 1946 with the refusal of the USSR to agree to the Baruch Plan for placing all nuclear technology, military and civil, under UN control. Then in 1948 came the communist coup d'état in Czechoslovakia, followed by the blockade of Berlin and, in 1949, by the explosion of the first Soviet atom bomb. There had been Korea, the defeat of the French in Indo-China; one incident after another that had made the Americans suspicious of, and determined to outbid, the USSR in military power. Fears of Soviet capabilities and intentions became acute when the first Sputnik was launched in 1957 and, correspondingly, the Russians became increasingly fearful of the intentions of the West. Warnings that the Soviet Union was well ahead of the USA in the size of their nuclear missile armoury, warnings of a so-called 'missile gap', which it is now known did not exist, started to be fostered, and became a powerful political card in the run-up to the 1960 presidential election which brought J. F. Kennedy to the White House. A race into space was launched. Throughout this period both the USA and the USSR were testing nuclear warheads in the atmosphere, with the UK participating on its own, but to a lesser extent.

In broad outline, this was the scene within which presidential science advisers and, to a lesser extent, the top advisers in the UK, faced their most serious test. There are many published records of what happened, but I would refer here particularly to the writings of Killian,[79] President Eisenhower's first Science Adviser; to those of Kistiakowsky,[80] his second; of Wiesner,[81] President Kennedy's Adviser; and of York.[24]

The original idea had been a ban on all nuclear tests, a goal for which the UK, which was also a party to the negotiations with the Soviet Union, had been striving. Like Harold Macmillan, this was also what President Eisenhower and then President Kennedy wanted — as I know at first hand, and especially through the direct exchanges I was engaged in at the time with the two main Presidential Science Advisers, Kistiakowsky and Wiesner. Obviously there was no direct knowledge, but Mr Macmillan certainly believed that Khrushchev had the same goal in mind.

Unfortunately there was also acute opposition to any treaty. Regardless of the worldwide and, from the scientific point of view, thoroughly justified concern about fallout, there were in fact many, including prominent scientists in the weapons laboratories of both the USA and the UK, who were opposed to even a ban on atmospheric tests, let alone an end to the elaboration of new warheads. One of the professional members of the Atomic Energy Commission of the USA, Willard F. Libby, a physicist, went so far as to say that,[82] 'the natural radioactivities of the body, the effects of the cosmic radiation and the natural radiation of the radioactivities of the earth's surface constitute hazards which are much greater than the test fallout hazards'. Such hawkish and scientifically fallacious views carried considerable weight among the military, in Congressional committees, and in some sections of the public, who soon became persuaded that there was something to be gained by continuing the nuclear arms race.

All the scientists and technical men who took part in the talks recognised that tests either in the atmosphere or in the seas could not pass undetected. Equally, those who wanted tests to continue could not deny that the seismic disturbances caused by very high-yield underground nuclear explosions could be differentiated from those due to earthquakes. But this, it was also understood, was not the case with disturbances caused by low-yield nuclear charges. Since the USSR, the Americans argued, was bound to cheat and carry out surreptitious underground tests, the Russians would have to agree to on-site inspections, that is to say to visits by teams of Americans to make sure that a seismic disturbance with its focal point in, say, a remote part of the USSR, was due to a 'natural event' such as an earthquake, and was not the result of an underground explosion. But the Russians had made it clear that they would agree to only a very few inspections. Such indications as they gave about the small number that would be acceptable to them, the American test enthusiasts ruled out as being insufficient to eliminate cheating. Nor was it safe, the argument went, for the USA to agree to a threshold of yield above which underground tests were forbidden. Even the lowest explosive yields which generate underground shock waves that cannot be differentiated from natural disturbances might have military significance. What was more, by testing in large underground cavities, whether natural or man-made, and not at the bottom of a very deep shaft, the shock wave caused by the explosion would be 'decoupled' from the walls of the cavity and, as a result, what might have been the explosion of a high-yield nuclear device would be made to seem a trivial affair. Having mastered the art of ballistic rocketry, the Russians might even carry out tests on the other side of the moon. And so the argument went on.

In July 1959, Harold Macmillan wrote[19] that: 'The Americans. . . seem now to be turning *against* a comprehensive agreement (to include underground tests). This, if true, is tragic.' Later he noted:[19] 'The real reason is that the Atomic Commission and the Pentagon are very keen to go on *indefinitely* with experiments (large and small) so as to keep refining upon and perfecting the art of nuclear weapons.' As he understood it, the Pentagon insisted that the Americans should continue testing underground partly because they wanted to devise a small 'tactical' weapon, to be used at one thousand yards range; partly for the 'anti-missile' missile, which to Mr Macmillan seemed 'almost a fantasy' — as it still is. During his talks with President Eisenhower in August 1959, Mr Macmillan expressed himself strongly.[19] 'I told [the] President that we ought to take risks for so great a prize. We might be blessed by future ages as saviours of mankind, or we might be cursed like the man who made' — quoting from Dante's *Inferno* — ' "*il gran rifiuto*" ' — the 'great refusal' made by Pope Celestine V when he abdicated from the papacy and so opened the way to Boniface, who, according to Dante, brought moral disaster on Church and Christendom.

Since it soon became apparent that there was no chance that the Senate would ratify a treaty for a total ban on testing unless the Russians accepted the condition of on-site inspection — which they had made plain they would not do — President Kennedy then had to settle for one which did not preclude underground testing[83]. As York writes,[24] 'one of the political prices' that the President had to pay in order to secure Congressional support for the Partial Test-Ban Treaty of 1963 was a promise that the

Atomic Energy Commission would embark on a programme of underground tests vigorous enough 'to satisfy all our military requirements'.

Because of the nature of the British parliamentary system, Mr Macmillan was in a position to overrule any opposition there might have been in the UK to a total ban — to which, in any event, there was none from any parliamentary quarter. But he, too, had to yield to the political pressures that were playing on President Kennedy. Regardless of the fact that the UK was a full, even if junior, partner in the negotiations, and despite other considerations, the constraints which the American legislature could impose on presidential power by virtue of the US Constitution affected the British Prime Minister as well as the President.

One reason why the Americans were so keen on continuing to test nuclear warheads was that by the time there was talk about test bans, they had already embarked on a vigorous programme to develop ballistic missiles. The Russians, not surprisingly, responded by intensifying theirs. This added another dimension to the arms race, as did the dream of devising anti-ballistic missile systems. In spite of the check imposed by SALT I on the latter idea, the opposing nuclear arsenals have continued to increase in size. Today the declared purpose of SALT II is to establish a measure of nuclear equivalence between the two sides, but clearly at a level which, were the present state of mutual deterrence ever to break down, would be well above the threshold needed to devastate utterly and without hope of repair, all the cities, even many of the small towns, of both the North American and Eurasiatic Continents, with hundreds of millions being killed in a flash, and with most of those who were not lucky enough to be among the dead then dying of the effects of radiation, of starvation, without medical or any other help. As I have said, the Russians are as much aware as we are of these grim realities. Yet however excessive the Western and Eastern nuclear arsenals already seem, today it looks as though the price that will have to be paid for the ratification of the SALT II treaty — given that it is ever ratified — is going to be another vast increase of expenditure by both sides on 'strategic nuclear systems' and on 'defence' generally.

How effective, then, were the chief scientific advisers as this scene unfolded? I would say not very. But it may well be that present prospects would be worse than they are had the advisers not been there. We might not have had even a partial test-ban — which many cynics now describe, not as an agreement which related to the arms race, but as the first international law to prohibit environmental pollution. But in general we all failed. In 1964, a year after the Partial Test-Ban Treaty was signed, York and Wiesner, who were associated with Presidents Eisenhower and Kennedy at the centre of the debate, published the article[29] to which I have already referred, and in which they stated that in assuring national security further tests of nuclear weapons were unnecessary. As they saw it, the increase in military power which might follow from further testing and from the elaboration of more nuclear weapons was bound, in both the East and the West, to bring about a decrease in national security. In the considered professional judgment of these two men — and they had all the facts at their disposal — a continuation of the nuclear arms race provided no escape from this curious paradox. This conclusion, which York later elaborated in his book *Race to Oblivion*,[24] is one to which in all logic I had been driven at the start of my career as Chief Scientific Adviser. Harold Brown, York's successor in the Pentagon as Director of Defense Research and Engineering, was of the same mind:[24]

'Those who have served as civilian officials in the Department of Defense at the level of Presidential appointment ... have recognized the severely limited utility of military power, and the great risks in its use, as well as the sad necessity of its possession ... [The] higher their position and, hence, their responsibility, the more they have come to the conclusion that we must seek national security through other than strictly military means ... and urgently.'

The state of the world has become much more perilous since the men whose words I have cited were in positions from which it would be assumed that they could have influenced events. Dr Hornig, who succeeded Dr Wiesner as Presidential Science Adviser, has written[84] that he was not in the inner circle of White House advisers who were concerned with national security matters. Nor, when President Nixon was elected, were the two scientists who succeeded him. When Henry Kissinger negotiated on technical matters on behalf of the President, he did not call on the strategic advice of scientists of the calibre of Wiesner. As an unfortunate consequence, his efforts to promote world peace, particularly during the negotiations that led up to the two Strategic Arms Limitation Treaties, allowed discussion of nuclear weaponry to be translated into numerical terms that have no meaning in the context of the potential destructive power of nuclear weapons — except perhaps to those who are not ill-disposed to the continuation of the nuclear arms race. What are essentially simple issues had become 'horrendously complex', as one experienced defence correspondent has recently put it.

It is, of course, possible that the upshot of the SALT negotiations would have been the same if a Wiesner or a Kistiakowsky had sat at Kissinger's side. Nonetheless, professional politicians are only too often under a handicap when dealing with scientific or technological matters. Only extremely rarely would one find in the office of Secretary of State for Defense anyone as well qualified for the post as was Harold Brown in President Carter's administration. His experience in one of the USA's two nuclear weapons laboratories, then as Director of Defense Research and Engineering, then as Secretary of the Air Force, plus what he gained as head of a famous university in the years when he was not part of the governmental machine, equipped him fully to deal with the myriad of technical problems and demands that reached his desk. He was able, when head of Defense, to protest that billions of dollars were being wasted in the name of US security because of vested political and industrial interests. One might well ask how many other political chiefs of defence departments are ever likely to be able to judge such matters on the basis of their own experience. Few indeed in the American system, and fewer still in the British. As Harold Macmillan has put it,[19]

'In all these affairs Prime Ministers, Ministers of Defence and Cabinets are under a great handicap. The technicalities and uncertainties of the sophisticated weapons which they have to authorise are out of the range of normal experience. There is today a far greater gap between their own knowledge and the expert advice which they receive than there has ever been in the history of war.'

This, perhaps, is one of the reasons why so little real progress has been made in the international negotiations that have been going on almost continuously since the conclusion of the 1963 Treaty.

The most recent round of negotiations to agree a comprehensive ban (CTB), laboriously pursued in Geneva on the instigation of President Carter from the summer of 1977, and now in suspense, achieved much at the technical level, but little when it came to the critical issue of what threshold of tests should still be allowed by a CTB. In an interesting article that was published in 1976,[85] and which reviews most of the arguments that have surfaced in test-ban talks, Donald Brennan wrote: 'The weapon community which is (quite properly) not without significant political influence, is unlikely (apart from rare exceptions) to support actively any CTB whatever, but some important elements of it might reluctantly acquiesce in an ICTB [that is to say, an "inclusive" ban, to which all nuclear weapon states adhere] if this assurance is provided'.

He was right. President Carter's original intention was to conclude an enduring comprehensive test ban, but he gradually gave way under pressure from the weapons community and its friends. The term of the ban which was politically possible for him became reduced, first to seven, then to five, and then to three years. All the old arguments were trundled out in public hearings held by the Congressional Committees through which pressure could be brought to bear on the President. It was claimed that the USA dared not risk a long ban on tests since it was necessary to test stockpiled weapons from time to time. In public testimony this assertion turned out to be technically incorrect. The cynic might well have asked what would be done if stockpiled weapons were tested and one failed 'to go off properly'. Test them all? Harold Agnew, then the Director of the Los Alamos nuclear laboratories, was luke-warm about any treaty that precluded low-yield tests, and joined the argument in favour of a ban of three years. Earlier he had put himself on public record to the effect that the USA's nuclear armoury would not suffer if there were no testing for ten years. As he put it,[86] 'I expect that with ample money, no restrictions on materials, and adequate non-nuclear testing, the stockpile could be maintained for a period of at least 10 years. However, stockpile problems do arise, as they have in the past, and in time there may be no experienced personnel available to assess the severity of the problems or with a background adequate to provide a fix if one is indeed possible. In addition there are examples in the past where the fix has required nuclear testing.'

Questions about monitoring suspicious seismic events had to be dealt with, for there were always American weapon experts who returned to the argument that even the smallest test could have military value; for example, by improving the yield/weight ratio of a warhead, or the efficiency of a 'primary' or trigger mechanism of a fusion bomb, or the possibilities of devising a small ABM warhead, or some tactical nuclear weapon. Seismic monitoring of suspicious events by what were called 'national technical means' was regarded as essential in order to 'enhance confidence' that no state party to the Treaty was cheating. But the bomb enthusiasts then argued that it would never be possible to be sure that a seismic disturbance of such and such a magnitude had not been caused by a low-yield, say a 3-kt, warhead. If one side could cheat to that level, all should be allowed to test to that level.

The argument became meaningless for, in the final analysis, those who wanted testing to go on might well have remained unsatisfied until it became possible to differentiate the seismic disturbances due to an explosion made by a few sticks of dynamite in a quarry or a coalmine from those resulting from a small nuclear test. Another argument of the American bomb enthusiasts was that the Russians did not have as urgent a need for continuous testing because their designs were 'more robust' than the sophisticated American or British. One might have thought that since what the Soviet Union had produced was adequate enough to pose an 'unacceptable' threat to America, the right thing to have done was to take a leaf out of their book and make the Western warheads more robust. But no. The arguments were as they had always been. Most important was the consideration that, without testing, the morale and experience of the men in the weapons laboratories would decline to unacceptable levels. Whatever the political gains a CTB might achieve, they were less important than assuring the continuity of the weapons laboratories. Herbert York, who led the American delegation at the recent round of CTB talks in Geneva, saw his brief becoming more hawkish as the months passed, and yet he knew that the weapons laboratories had 'made no significant breakthroughs since Teller and other scientist-experts put forth their claims in the early 1960s that new advances were just around the corner'.[82] The nuclear balance had not been affected in any way by refinements in warhead design.

A final obstacle then revealed itself. If a ban of a few years were agreed, the agreement would have to be reviewed at the end of the period. The Soviet Union wanted it to be understood that testing would not be resumed unless the political circumstances had altered dramatically. But the pressures that had built up in the United States were working in an opposite direction. Many of the American technical experts wanted a tacit understanding that testing would be resumed at the end of the agreed period, whatever the political circumstances.

The futility of negotiating against a background of such contradictory aims does not need underlining. It becomes absurd when one realises that, were nuclear war to erupt any time in the next decade, it would make no difference at all what the Russians or the Americans or the British did to their nuclear arsenals or defences in the meantime. Whether they increased their size, or added new designs, it would not make the slightest difference either to the extent or the intensity of the devastation which North America, Europe, and at least the western half of the USSR would suffer.

CHAPTER 8

What Next?

The Defense Budget submitted by President Carter to Congress stood at approximately $170 billion for the year 1981, equal to about half the Gross National Product of the United Kingdom. Almost immediately after assuming office, President Reagan asked Congress to agree a further $30 billion, and a figure of $220 billion has been mooted for the fiscal year 1982. It is likely to be agreed. The military build-up that is being proposed is three times as large as the one that took place during the years of the Vietnam War, and it is argued that this is bound to have a highly damaging effect on the whole US economy,[87] partly because of the competition that must occur between the defence and civil sectors for scarce materials and trained manpower, and partly because so large an increase in defence spending without any rise in taxation cannot but lead to rapid inflation.

Whether President Reagan's many economic critics are proved right or wrong, we can be sure that all this additional expenditure, given that it materialises, will not be adding *pro rata* to America's 'security'. If the history of the post-war arms race is any guide, the extra money is likely to reduce it. That the Russians will react by adding to the resources they devote to defence can be taken for granted, for that has been their usual response. The net effect will be that the dangers of political and military misadventure, or nuclear accident, will increase even above their present levels. There have already been enough false alarms due to malfunctioning of radars and computers in early-warning systems, and enough unresolved political and military clashes which could escalate into open conflict that would affect the super-powers directly. If, in a few years, bilateral or trilateral SALT negotiations are resumed, the cliché of 'negotiating from strength' will again be seen to be as empty as it has proved in the past. Adding to defence outlays in order to have more 'bargaining chips' that can be 'traded' in future negotiations relating to arms control has proved a worthless enterprise. In 1971, during the course of the SALT I talks, Henry Kissinger admitted[23] — presumably with the authority of the President he represented — that there was no longer any such thing as 'nuclear superiority'. He may not have been consistent over the years in his pronouncements on nuclear matters, but he could not have been more to the point on that occasion. Ten years later, after both sides have added substantially to their nuclear arsenals, neither enjoys any superiority. Both armouries have long since passed the level that would be necessary to assure overwhelming mutual destruction.

Only political determination based upon an understanding of what are the immutable facts of destruction can break the deadlock of the nuclear arms race. The arguments of nuclear weapons technicians are the natural reaction of men with a vested interest in the pursuit of their patriotic duties. But the concept of nuclear war is nonetheless a nonsense, unless there exist political goals for the United States, or for Western Europe, or for the Warsaw Pact powers of such inestimable value that their attainment justifies the price of annihilation. Of course, there would be some survivors from a nuclear holocaust, but what would they be doing in a destroyed world ?

By the end of the fifties, and certainly by the early sixties, there were many who, recognizing the enormous destructive power of thermonuclear weapons, realized that a state of nuclear parity already prevailed between the USA and the USSR. That was certainly Harold Macmillan's view, and McGeorge Bundy tells us[20] that it was also a view which President Kennedy shared. He also cites Carl Kaysen, a senior member of the National Security Council in President Kennedy's day, and later Director of the Institute for Advanced Study at Princeton, who, in an article in 1968, wrote:[88] 'We cannot expect with any confidence to do more than achieve a secure second-strike capacity, no matter how hard we try. This capacity is not usefully measured by counting warheads or megatons or, above some level, expected casualties. Whether the result comes about with twice as many American as Soviet delivery vehicles — as has been the case in the past — or with roughly equal numbers, or even with an adverse ratio, does not change its basic nature.' Raymond Aron, the distinguished French political and strategic commentator, had said much the same thing in 1961.

Indeed, it has always been the only rational view. There is no sense in the belief that the enormous increase that has been made in the size of the nuclear arsenals of both sides since functional parity was achieved has reinforced the state of mutual deterrence. As Admiral G. E. Miller, a former deputy director of the US Joint Strategic Planning Staff, pointed out at a Pugwash Symposium held in Toronto in 1978, new nuclear warheads are not produced in answer to military demand; they are turned out and then have to be assigned targets, whether or not there is a requirement for additional destructive capacity.

No technical defence against a nuclear onslaught could possibly make political sense. ABM systems, particle beams, lasers in space, provide ample opportunity for fascinating and costly enquiry by engineering experts. But, as Dr Jack Ruina, a former director of the Pentagon's Advanced Research Projects Agency, and one of the foremost authorities on ABM systems, points out in a recent paper,[89] the chances of technical success are remote in the extreme. ABM systems are still pie in the sky for political leaders who would wish to be assured, before engaging in military adventures, that the price for so doing, in terms of the destruction which their countries would suffer, would not be catastrophic.

The world's leaders have declared that they want to see an end to the nuclear arms race. That this has not happened is due to the fact that the leadership in the USA and the USSR is fearful of taking action because the defence scientists and 'intelligence' experts who are at the heart of the race are always able to generate alarm about what the other side is doing, or may be doing. But this need not go on for ever. The success of SALT I, and the more limited success of SALT II, became possible because space surveillance and other techniques of intelligence allowed both sides to learn a great deal about each other's progress in the ABM race, and about the deployment of land-based missiles. On the other hand, while the new technologies can help inform the two sides of certain facts, I doubt if they could ever give either side the assurance it would want that it knew enough not only of its opponent's capabilities but, more important, of its intentions. The suspicion that exists in the West about the Soviet Union's expansionist intentions, and those which plague the USSR about the motives of the NATO powers, are certainly not going to be allayed through technological developments.

Satellite photography, whether visual or infra-red, has improved out of all recognition in barely a decade. Space photographs processed by digitalisation and intensification, using computers, now have a resolution that makes it possible to monitor troop movements, the location of gun and silo emplacements, the occurrence of earth disturbances, of crop failures and forest blight. But on their own they cannot be expected to generate a sufficient sense of security to either side. The whereabouts of the Soviet mobile SS20 MIRVed missile can be determined at any moment. The SS20, however, is a missile that can be reloaded. So there are doubts. Are those launchers that can be seen in such and such a place in a state of readiness ? Or are they not ? Photographs will not tell. Space cameras cannot see into factories where missiles are made, or into the sheds of ship-yards. Photographs cannot tell whether stacks of drums outside an assumed chemical-warfare plant contain nerve-gas or oil, or whether they are empty. Space photographs will provide a map of a terrain more accurate than any that have been constructed from ordnance surveys, and so make it possible to determine with precision the coordinates of desired aiming points for ballistic or cruise missiles. But since accuracy is measured in terms of CEP, they do not make it possible to predict where the fifty per cent of shots that will on average fall outside the CEP radius will strike.

The objective of military intelligence has always been to try and deduce from all possible sources the capabilities and intentions of a potential enemy. New technology has certainly added to what we know about the first, but it has hardly improved our abilities in the second. How much did it help in Vietnam ? Why did Afghanistan come as such a surprise ? Is the West now drawing the right conclusions about Soviet intentions from pictures and reports of troop concentrations on the borders of Poland? Being able to see what is happening on the other side of the hill achieves a real value only when one knows what an enemy is about to do, or is likely to do. And there science does not help.

Nor is it likely that new science or technology could ever bring political certainty to the monitoring of arms-control agreements, any more than it is likely to play a positive part in bringing about such agreement. Whatever information new sensor techniques, whether visual, thermal, acoustic or seismic provide, it is almost certain that it will not lend itself to interpretation in simple black and white terms. Indeed, the development of new devices for gathering information is more likely to exacerbate divisions in the scientific community between those who will interpret the evidence as indicating that the other side is cheating, and those who take the contrary view. The enthusiasts of both sides will argue that they be allowed to continue with their own attempts to develop new weapons because they are sure that their potential enemy is gaining some arcane advantage from something it is thought he is doing.

Harold Macmillan once observed that politicians have to run hard to catch up with the scientists. But if their goal is peace, then politicians are in the wrong race. The scientists who work in the defence departments of governments, or in defence industries, are not apostles of peace. Political and military leaders should cease seeking shelter behind the backs of those 'experts' who take what is usually called the harder line. In the twenty years since the first major effort was made to bring the nuclear arms race to an end, masses of water have flowed under the bridge. If the bridge itself is not to become submerged, the politicians will have to take charge of the technical men.

This will not be easy. Whatever the President of the United States may want to see happen, he has to carry the Senate with him. The Senators, in turn, are under pressure from military chiefs, from industry, and from their constituents. And while the military chiefs may have to defer to the President as their commander in chief, they also have their own constituents to deal with: the men below them in the service hierarchies, and in the industries to which part of the defence vote is always committed. I do not know what the position is in the USSR, and what influence the Soviet military may have on the Secretary of the Party and on the Central Committee. In the United Kingdom we are relatively fortunate. The Prime Minister, with the majority party behind him, has all the authority he or she needs to take decisions where national security is concerned. In 1960 Harold Macmillan was personally committed to the achievement of a comprehensive test ban. As I have said, in declaring his position publicly, it was not necessary for him to seek the assent either of his Chiefs of Staff or of the heads of the country's weapons laboratories.

It will take years before the great powers start living in peace. They never will unless several other things happen first. Above all, the nuclear threat must be reduced, and for that to come about the goal should be a halt to all R and D designed to elaborate new nuclear warheads and new means of delivery. Correspondingly, an effort should be made to end all work, vain as it is, to devise ABM defences. Even if such systems could never prove significant in the reduction of 'unacceptable' destruction, suspicion is generated by the fact that R and D to devise such systems (and counter-systems) continues. As a result the nuclear balance becomes 'destabilised'.

It should be recognised that ending R and D in the field of nuclear weapons would make no difference whatever to the capabilities of nations to fight wars. Were anything material to result from any new R and D or any R and D in progress, it would merely create grounds for political argument ten years hence, as the Soviet SS20 is doing today. The SS20 started to be deployed in 1977. Unless the Russians are much smarter than either the Americans or the British, its life on the drawing board could not have begun any later than about 1967, when the cold war was at its most frigid. Then, not now, would have been the time to start negotiations for a 'balanced reduction' in nuclear armaments, including the cessation of work on the SS20, in the same way as the time to nip the MIRV concept in the bud was the late sixties. When the SALT II talks were opened, it was already far too late for that. Not that the advent of the SS20 now means that European cities are threatened for the first time. They have always been targeted, not only by Soviet aircraft, but also by IRBMs.

Neither the ABM issue nor that of theatre nuclear weapons would have arisen if the test ban talks of the early sixties had ended in a comprehensive ban rather than one limited to only two 'environments'. The fact is that the number of underground tests of nuclear warheads that both sides have conducted since 1963 far exceeds the number that were carried out before in the atmosphere and the seas. And far from the continued testing having enhanced the security of the super-powers, the uninterrupted elaboration and multiplication of warheads and of the means of their delivery, have merely added to the peril in which the USA, the USSR, and the rest of us live.

If governments go on behaving as though they were the servants of those technical and military advisers who have a vested interest in seeing that there should be no test ban treaty, there never will be a treaty. One will be concluded only when the political leaders of the two sides, realising that changes in the yield or design of some particular weapon, of the kind that called for a test, could make no conceivable difference to the deterrent status of their countries, determine that it should be. As David Owen fully recognized when he was the UK's Foreign Secretary,[90] a comprehensive test ban is a *sine qua non* if the suspicions which the non-nuclear states entertain about those that already have nuclear arsenals are to be allayed. In 1985, when the Non-Proliferation Treaty again comes up for review, the non-nuclear states will have every reason to condemn the nuclear powers for the vertical proliferation in which they have been engaged over the past fifteen years.

Given the political will, a comprehensive ban should not

be a difficult treaty to agree. The indications, however, are that President Reagan is in no hurry to resume negotiations, and it is clear that the priority of a CTB is well behind that of SALT — as indeed was becoming the case in the last years of President Carter's regime. Some powerful senators on whom the ratification of a CTB treaty would depend are not even yet persuaded that a ban on further tests is essential if the nuclear arms race is to be curbed. It is, however, a fact of history that with every delay in reaching an agreement on the control of nuclear arms, nuclear weapons change and build up so fast that the best that could be achieved later is worse than the worst that might have been concluded a year or two before. Henry Kissinger once recognised this. He probably still does. With every delay our mutual peril becomes greater. If, therefore, it is no longer an urgent interest of the United States to bring about a comprehensive test ban, the initiative should, in my view, be taken by the European nuclear powers, and by those non-nuclear members of NATO who are opposed to the deployment of new nuclear weapons, and who have become hostages in the nuclear arms race, not its beneficiaries. And if political realities reveal that agreement between the super-powers is impossible unless a threshold level of tests were allowed, so be it. A treaty which permitted underground tests up to a yield of, say, 2 kt, would be better than no treaty at all. For without even a low threshold ban there can be no reality to the Non-Proliferation Treaty.

Talk of a balanced reduction of forces — to which all sides are committed — will remain mere words until a presumptive CTB is successfully negotiated. There is also the question of what meaning should be attached to the concept of 'balanced' reduction. The SALT II negotiations dragged on until reality disappeared behind a smokescreen of calculations, and of comparisons of the total 'throw-weight' of the armouries of the two sides, and so on. The upshot was an agreement which left both sides with enough nuclear weapons and delivery systems to blow each other apart several times over, whether this were done in the name of retaliation, or of posthumous revenge, or in the pursuit of euphemisms such as 'countervalue' and 'counterforce' policies (which, in the end, mean the same thing).

The successful achievement of SALT I is an indication of what could be done, given the political will, backed by more of the simple kind of question that President Johnson posed about ABMs — will it or will it not work. If rational discussion and sensible compromise cannot sort out political differences, nuclear war certainly won't. The acute suspicions which the West and East entertain about each other's nuclear capabilities must be replaced by the understanding that in the final analysis it would be utterly irrational for either side to risk total destruction in order to further some political interest which is hostile to the other.

It will not be easy to devise adequate machinery to assure the goal of halting R and D on nuclear weapons. But that it can be done I have no doubt, given only that the task of monitoring a slow-down leading to a halt is not entrusted to those who either have, or who have had, a vested interest in preventing such a thing. As the disclosures about the start of the Chevaline and Trident programmes in the United Kingdom illustrate, a great deal can happen behind the shutters of defence research establishments without the knowledge of those who are either responsible for policy or for the provision of the necessary resources.

Admittedly, the efforts that have so far been made to slow down the nuclear arms race have proved all but fruitless. If future attempts are to succeed, there will have to be a general recognition that from the point of view of deterrence nothing would be lost if the size of the nuclear arsenals of both sides were significantly reduced. Britain and France hold that the nuclear armaments which they deploy, and which are only a fraction the size of those of the USA and the USSR, are adequate to constitute independent deterrent forces. Either the two small European nuclear powers are living in a dream world, or the level of forces which the unratified SALT II agreement allowed the two super-powers to maintain is miles in excess of what would be necessary to restrain either from military action directly inimical to the other.

I would not for a moment pretend that the concept of minimal deterrence which, as McGeorge Bundy reminds us[46], was unwelcome to the Americans — partly, I believe, because it was advanced at a time when their nuclear armoury was being vastly extended — is what has determined the size of the British and French nuclear forces. That is far more likely to have been decided by the volume of resources which could be made available. But the reality remains. Whether or not the British Polaris boats would ever be used 'independently', the United Kingdom has what is termed an independent nuclear force, and the proposition that it is big enough to deter is, in my view, unassailable. The decision to replace Polaris with Trident, which would mean, because of MIRV, increasing the number of warheads each missile carries, makes no logical difference to this basic proposition.

Why then is it necessary for the Russians and Americans to maintain nuclear forces that are fifty to a hundred times bigger ?

There is another set of considerations which seems strangely illogical. The state of mutual nuclear deterrence which prevails between the Warsaw Pact and NATO powers may well have helped keep the peace in Europe these past thirty years, but the best military opinion now concedes that, were any nuclear weapons ever to be used in a 'theatre context', that is to say, used in, or in support of, field warfare, the likelihood is overwhelming that the conflict would rapidly escalate to an all-out nuclear exchange. The 'new' weapons that are spoken about, the SS20s, cruise missiles, Pershing IIs and neutron bombs, thus add little significant to the threat already faced by the West on the one hand, and by the USSR and its satellites on the other. More 'theatre' weapons might mean that more targets would be hit, but it would be ridiculous to suppose that those which are the most important, and these include the capitals of the NATO countries, are not already targeted, in the same way as those in Warsaw Pact territory, which would be pre-targeted for cruise missiles or Pershing IIs, are not already marked for destruction. From the start it was illogical to exclude from the SALT II negotiations the 'forward-based' nuclear systems which theatre and tactical nuclear weapons comprise. How can there be any logic in separating such weapons from those in the 'strategic' armoury when the chances are so great that any nuclear weapon, whether it is called tactical, or theatre, or strategic, would trigger an all-out exchange ? It certainly would not matter to the smaller members of the NATO alliance if three or four nuclear weapons which had devastated their territory were later designated by the Russians to have been 'tactical' rather than 'strategic'.

Since a strategic nuclear exchange, whether started deliberately or triggered by accident, would almost certainly become unrestrained, and since the likelihood is that a 'theatre' or 'field' exchange would end the same way, it is surely right that if the SALT process is ever restarted, it should take into its orbit all, not just some, nuclear weapon systems. SALT should become the NALT negotiations — if we are going to continue using acronyms — the nuclear arms limitation talks.

However they are restarted, negotiations need to be governed by only a few basic propositions: first, that the chances are that any nuclear exchange would escalate to the point of mutual annihilation; second, that no practicable active defences such as ABMs exist against nuclear weapons, or are on the horizon, or could be afforded, even if in a limited way only, by any countries other than the USA and the USSR (which would leave London, Paris, Rome, Bonn, Brussels, and other cities to be advertised as defenceless); and third, that the scale of the nuclear forces deployed in Britain and France be taken as a yardstick of what size of nuclear forces are enough to deter in a bilateral context.

Any new round of negotiations should begin by focusing, not on those weapon systems that can strike directly at the United States or the USSR, but on the nuclear warheads, whether designated tactical or theatre, which are deployed by the Warsaw Pact and NATO powers, and whose use would be likely to trigger an all-out exchange. It should be far easier to reach agreement at this level, which acutely concerns the security of all European countries, whether or not members of NATO or of the Warsaw Pact, than in further bargaining about strategic systems that are already more than adequate to blow the two super-powers, and the rest of the northern industrialised world, into oblivion. Negotiations about these strategic systems could well wait until the situation which could trigger their use is defused.

Moreover, neither the USA's nor the USSR's present negotiating position would be strengthened by adding still further to the size and variety of their respective arsenals (each of which represents far more destructive power than the rest of the armouries of the world put together). Adding more would be akin to doubling the dose of a poison, for which there is no antidote, which was already ten times above the lethal level. Without either side lowering its guard, there is therefore no logical reason why the USSR and the USA should wait until they cease to suspect each other's intentions before they start the process of bilaterally reducing their battlefield nuclear forces. In a rational world, a state of political détente would not be a necessary condition for a start to the process of a 'balanced reduction' of nuclear arms, although a political détente would certainly help.

The failure of the disarmament talks of the past thirty years to achieve any significant results has led in several countries to campaigns for unilateral disarmament, a term which is normally taken to imply unilateral nuclear disarmament. In the United Kingdom this goal was once, and is again, officially part of the political platform of the Labour Party although, when in power, which means 23 of the 36 postwar years, it took no steps to implement its declared policy (some might regard it as ironical that it was a Labour Government which decided that Britain should become an independent nuclear power). Aneurin Bevan, one of the most significant and engaging of Labour politicians, and a man whose death transformed British politics, once upheld the cause of unilateral disarmament, in contrast to Hugh Gaitskell, the leader of his party and, for a time, his bitter opponent. When the two became reconciled, Bevan, to the dismay of his admirers and followers, argued at the 1957 Labour Party conference against unilateral nuclear disarmament, declaring[91] that were the Labour Party to achieve power on the basis of such a policy, it would be sending a Foreign Secretary, whoever he might be, 'naked into the conference chamber'. 'We want to have the opportunity', he went on to say, 'of interposing between the two giants, modifying, moderating, and mitigating influence . . . it is not just a question of who is in favour of the hydrogen bomb, but a question of what is the most effective way of getting the damn thing destroyed.'

Had a reliable clairvoyant been present to foretell the value the British nuclear arsenal would have in assuring the UK's position in the world, or whether it would help arrest the decline in the UK's economic and political power, I wonder if Bevan would have made his plea. Britain's possession of nuclear weapons has not yet made any obvious difference to the effectiveness of her voice in the conference chamber, where at times she has certainly been outshone by others who do not belong to the nuclear club.

But even if the possession of nuclear weapons has not yet yielded the influence which Aneurin Bevan hoped for, there are powerful reasons why Britain should not espouse the cause of unilateral disarmament. I say this at the same time as I respect the sincerity of many who, like E. P. Thompson, are now in the forefront of the organised movement to bring about unilateral disarmament. I do not have in mind the moral argument, to which there can be no answer. I am fully sensitive to the moral objections to weapons of mass destruction.

Nuclear weapons exist. The knowledge of how to make them exists, and cannot be made to vanish. The United Kingdom contributed greatly to the success of the scientific and technological effort which produced the first nuclear weapons. We may now be overshadowed and perhaps disregarded by the two super-powers, but we are nonetheless a founder member of the nuclear weapons club. These are the basic facts. What I cannot see is the practical benefit of abandoning what we have, whereas I do see certain disadvantages.

First, it is claimed that were we to abandon or even reduce our relatively small armoury (small in terms of number, not in that of destructive power), others would follow suit, at the same time as some countries which might otherwise go nuclear would, as a result of the United Kingdom's example, desist from such a step. The question that needs to be asked is, which countries ? Surely not the USA and the USSR, who will clearly decide their policies with respect to levels of disarmament between themselves, and not in response to any gesture that the UK alone might make ? Had NATO's forward-based systems not been totally separated from strategic systems in the SALT negotiations — as though tactical and strategic were different, either in terms of yield, or range, or effects — the position might have been otherwise. But they were separated, and we were not in the conference chamber.

A second reason — among others — that is advanced in favour of unilateral disarmament is that were we to divest ourselves of our nuclear weapons, we would be less likely to be a target in the event of a nuclear war. This is wishful thinking. Were such a war ever to erupt, we would still be part of NATO, and in the light of presumed Soviet military doctrine, it would be idle to suppose that we would be immune from attack. Associated with this idea is the mounting opposition both in the United Kingdom and in other NATO countries to the proposal to station here the two new American nuclear weapon systems: cruise and Pershing II. As I understand it, the argument — again, apart from the moral issue — is that deploying these new systems would accelerate the nuclear arms race, at the same time as it would make it all the more likely that the countries that accepted the new weapons would become targets in case of nuclear attack. I can see point in the first argument, but none in the second. Were nuclear weapons ever to be used in a war between the NATO and Warsaw Pact powers, we would all be targets. We would all be destroyed. Moreover, not even neutral Switzerland or neutral Sweden would be immune from the effects of a nuclear exchange on the European mainland. Fallout and the dislocation of production and communications in other countries would affect all — some obviously more than others — but nonetheless all. Those who go further and argue that the United Kingdom should withdraw from NATO should ask themselves, what then ? Whatever its military value, our withdrawal from NATO would force all the Continental powers, including the United Kingdom, either independently or as part of the European Economic Community, to come to terms with the USSR. Henry Kissinger has always been an ardent supporter of NATO, and he is certainly no conventional American isolationist. Again, one should remember his 1979 remark[45] that the European allies of the United States should not keep asking the USA 'to multiply strategic assurances that we cannot possibly mean or if we do mean, we should not want to execute because if we execute we risk the destruction of civilization'.

Some unilateralists might, of course, argue that were European states to come to terms with the USSR separately and independently of the USA, in the acceptance of her right to try to make her socialist world and that of her allies flourish — even to spread her influence — this would be preferable to the prospect of nuclear war. This is not an issue which is relevant to the argument of this book.

On the positive side, there is another reason why the UK should retain its nuclear arsenal, and which, to the best of my knowledge has never been deployed. Paradoxically, its continued possession could help in the process of world disarmament, not because the UK might be allowed to argue the case in the conference chamber, but because the scale of what it has, and what the French have, is an indication to the two super-powers of the forces that are adequate to maintain a deterrent threat. The Americans and the Russians have allowed themselves to be impelled blindly in a senseless nuclear arms race which has no finishing post. This is the message that should be broadcast, together with a corollary that nuclear parity or sufficiency, as Liddell Hart argued twenty years ago, leads to nuclear nullity; that there can be no such thing as nuclear superiority; that no country could regard a nuclear exchange as a realistic band in the spectrum of military options. In 1950, when Truman was President, the idea of using nuclear weapons in Korea was considered, when MacArthur's forces were driven back from the Yalu. Mr Attlee went to see the President to dissuade him, and for that, and no doubt other reasons, the plan was rejected. The same thing happened in 1954, during the Eisenhower administration, when the question of using nuclear weapons to raise the siege of Dien Bien Phu was debated. In that case Winston Churchill intervened. In February 1968 the Americans engaged in a 'brief but heated flurry of debate' over the desirability of using nuclear weapons to raise the siege of Khe Sanh during the Vietnam war — but again desisted.[92] Both the USA and the USSR recoiled from the idea of a nuclear exchange in the Cuban crisis. But at the same time there have been scores of wars since the advent of nuclear weapons. The nuclear arsenals of the great powers have not prevented them. Nuclear weapons and nuclear weapon systems are not weapons of war. Whenever their use has been contemplated, the idea has been abandoned. Not only are they not weapons of war, but the amount of military input into complex nuclear systems is all but minimal, with a complementary increase in the technical input provided by the non-military man. As I put it in 1962:[1] 'No military genius or experience went into the conception or design of inter-continental ballistic missiles. There is no logical need for such a weapon to be deployed by the military as opposed to some agent of government. If the name of Moscow or New York or London or Paris were written on each ICBM, the missiles might well be deployed and operated by the firms which produced them'. Today this applies just as much to cruise missiles, or Pershing IIs, or SS20s, as it did to the ICBMs of twenty years ago. Far from increasing the number of options open to the military man, nuclear weapon systems weigh him down. The contrivances and machinery of modern technology can be the enemy of military flexibility.

The United Kingdom has decided to 'up-date' or 'modernise' its nuclear armoury. If this is something the country can afford, it will make, as I have said, little difference to her deterrent status; it will not increase the 'credibility' of her deterrent force. It will hardly make the Russians more fearful of the UK tomorrow than they are today, any more than there is cause for a rational UK citizen to be more fearful of Soviet nuclear power today than he was twenty years ago, by when the United Kingdom could already have been wiped out in a single blow. If the argument is that the UK's present Polaris submarines will have 'worn out' by 1990, and that she needs to continue as a nuclear power to the year 2000 and beyond, then I would say that we should despair for the Western world if by that time discussion and negotiations about East-West and North-South political and economic relations have not taken on a less warlike tone. Nor can I imagine that the possession of a few Trident missile submarines will help Britain to discover a new role in the world to replace that which she enjoyed when she still had a vast empire, to echo the hurtful gibe made by the late Dean Acheson, the distinguished Secretary of State in Truman's administration.

The UK's nuclear effort makes sense only because its nuclear boats and aircraft are assigned to NATO within the implicit framework of the concept of minimal deterrence. Not for one second do I believe that it is Britain's nuclear power that deters the USSR from taking action so hostile to the UK's interests that it would be driven to independent nuclear action, any more than I believe that the democratic process accords any Western political leader — and our leaders do not usually achieve power because of the votes of a majority of the electorate — the right to initiate a nuclear war, and incinerate not only their share of the electorate, but also those by whom he or she may have been opposed. What would be left of Europe and the

USSR after an all-out nuclear exchange would not have been worth fighting for. Nor would there have been any justification for the price that the USA would have had to pay for coming to Europe's aid.

If the UK is to discover a new role in the nuclear world, if we are to resurrect the kind of international strategic influence that was last exercised, even if only with limited success, in the final years of Harold Macmillan's ministry, we shall need to remind ourselves continuously that if anything is going to inhibit the Russians from making any incursion into NATO Europe, it will be NATO's conventional forces; and that so long as détente is merely a word and not a process, such resources as NATO's European members can command should be devoted to strengthening these forces. Were the UK to improve and add to those that are already deployed in the defence of Europe, it would be certain to play a far more influential role in the defence of the free world than it now does. The technological skills that go to nuclear weapons could be used to increase the R and D that is devoted to conventional armaments. Such a move would do far more to add to the real military options open to NATO in fending off attack than could ever be done by increasing the number of weapons in the Western nuclear armoury, and all of which, whatever their nature, carry the risk of triggering an all-out nuclear war. The concept of nuclear deterrence, of nuclear parity, has no reality unless it is backed with adequate conventional forces. If one reads between the lines of what some Western intelligence experts and armchair nuclear strategists write about disparities in the numbers of troops we and our possible enemies deploy, this is something that is clearly understood by the Warsaw Pact powers.

REFERENCES

1   Zuckerman, S., 1962, Judgment and control in modern warfare, *Foreign Affairs,* 40(2), 196-212.
2   *Hansard,* House of Commons, 25 January 1962, Cols 401-403.
3   *quoted in* Bonnart, F., 1981, Dangers of reliance on nuclear arms, *The Times* (13 May).
4   Bradley, O.N., 1981, *The Defense Monitor,* 10(2), Washington, D.C.: Center for Defense Information (Report of speech at St. Alban's School, Washington, D.C., November 5, 1957).
5   *Hansard,* House of Commons, 28 April 1980, col. 1046.
6   Zuckerman, S., 1966, *Scientists and War,* London: Hamish Hamilton.
7   Craven, W.F., and Cate, J.L. (eds), 1953, *The Army Air Forces in World War II,* 5, Chicago: University of Chicago Press.
8   Smyth, H.D., 1945, *Atomic Energy,* Washington D.C.: US Government Printing Office; London: HMSO.
9   *Comprehensive Study on Nuclear Weapons,* 1980. Report of the Secretary-General to General Assembly of the United Nations.
10 Zuckerman, S., 1952, Vulnerability of human targets to fragmenting and blast weapons, *Textbook of Air Armament,* London: Ministry of Supply.
11 Glasstone, S. (ed), 1962, *The Effects of Nuclear Weapons,* Washington, D.C.: US Government Printing Office.
12 *Effects of the Possible Use of Nuclear Weapons,* 1968, Report of the Secretary General to the United Nations, New York.
13 *The Effects of Nuclear War,* 1979, Office of Technology Assessment, Washington, D.C.: US Government Printing Office.
14 Lewis, K.N., 1979, The prompt and delayed effects of nuclear war, *Scientific American,* 241(1), 27-39.
15 *quoted in* Reinhold, R., 1981. *International Herald Tribune* (24 March).
16 *Economic and Social Consequences of Nuclear Attacks on the United States,* 1979, Washington, D.C.: US Government Printing Office.
17 *The Effects of Nuclear War,* 1979, United States Arms Control and Disarmament Agency.
18 Hackett, Sir John, 1981, The best possible defence for Britain, *Sunday Telegraph* (24 May).

19 Macmillan, H., 1972, *Pointing the Way*, London: Macmillan.

20 Bundy, McGeorge, 1979, Strategic deterrence after thirty years (Keynote remarks at Annual Conference of International Institute for Strategic Studies, Villars, Switzerland).

21 Dulles, J.F., 1954, Address to Council of Foreign Relations, 12 January.

22 *Hansard*, House of Commons, March 1955, Cols. 1899-1900.

23 Kissinger's critique, 1979, *The Economist* (3 February), 17-22. see also, Kissinger, H. A., 1976, *International Security*, 1(1), 182-191.

24 York, H.F., 1970, *Race to Oblivion*, New York: Simon & Schuster.

25 *Defence. Outline of Future Policy*, 1957, London: HMSO (Cmnd 124).

26 GLC to scrap £1m nuclear contingency planning, 1981, *The Times* (21 May), 6.

27 Tsipis, K., 1981, *Directed Energy Weapons Feasibility and Effectiveness* (Paper presented at IFRI Colloq. Science and Disarmament, Paris, January).

   Parmentola, J., and K. Tsipis, 1979, Particle-beam weapons, *Scientific American*, 240(4), 38-49.

   Garwin, R.L., 1981, *Weapons in Space: Are we on the verge of a new arms race?* (Paper presented to AAAS Annual Meeting, Toronto, 3-8 January.)

28 Ellis, R.H., 1980, *Building a Plan for Peace*, Washington, D.C.: Joint Strategic Target Planning Staff.

29 Wiesner, J.B., and H.F. York, 1964, National security and the Nuclear Test Ban, *Scientific American*, 211(4).

30 Kissinger, H., 1960, *The Necessity for Choice*, London: Chatto.

31 Liddell Hart, B.H.,1960, *Deterrent or Defence*, London: Stevens & Sons.

32 *quoted in* 31 above.

33 Enthoven, A.C., 1975, US Forces in Europe: How many? Doing what? *Foreign Affairs*, 53(3), 513-532.

34 Mountbatten, Louis, 1979/80, A military commander surveys the nuclear arms race, *International Security*, 4(3), 3-5.

35 Hill-Norton, Lord, 1980, *The Times* (13 May) (Letter).

36 *Hansard*, House of Lords, 23 April 1980, Col. 843.

37 Cameron, Sir Neil, 1980, Defence in the 1990s, *J.Roy.Soc.Arts*, (August), pp.604-614.

38 Collins, A.S., 1979, How a nuclear war would be fought on land, *Bull. Atomic Scientists* (May), 28-30.

39 *International Herald Tribune*, 16 September 1980.

40 Schmidt, H., 1962, *Defence or Retaliation*, London: Oliver & Boyd.

41 Sokolovskii, V.D. (ed), 1968, *Military Strategy* (3rd edn), Moscow: Military Publishing House.

42 Brodie, B., 1947, in *The Absolute Weapon*, New York: Harcourt Brace, pp.21-110.

43 Brodie, B., 1978, The development of nuclear strategy, *International Security*, 2(4), 65-83.

44 Howard, M., 1979, The forgotten dimensions of strategy, *Foreign Affairs*, 57(5), 975-986.

45 *quoted in* Jobert, M., 1979, *International Herald Tribune* (22 October).

46 Bundy, McGeorge, 1978/79, Maintaining stable deterrence, *International Security*, 3(3), 5-16.

47 Foster, W.C., 1965, New directions in arms control and disarmament, *Foreign Affairs*, 43(4), 587-601.

48 Clark, R.W., 1980, *The Greatest Power on Earth*, London: Sidgwick & Jackson, p. 126.

49 Williams, F., 1961, *A Prime Minister Remembers*, London: Heinemann.

50 Acheson, Dean, 1969, *Present at the Creation*, New York: W.W. Norton.

51 Clark, R.W., 1980, *The Greatest Power on Earth*, London: Sidgwick & Jackson, p.234.

52 *The Future United Kingdom Strategic Nuclear Deterrent Force*, 1980, London: Ministry of Defence, Defence Open Government Document 80/23.

53 Wilson, H., 1971, *The Labour Government*, London: Weidenfeld & Nicolson.

54 Perry, W.J., 1981, *The FY 1982 Department of Defense Program for Research, Development and Acquisition* (Statement to the 97th US Congress First Session).

55 Long, F.A., and J. Reppy (eds), 1980, *The Genesis of New Weapons: Decision Making for Military R & D*, London: Pergamon.

56 Long, F.A., 1980, *The Process of New Weapons Development* (Paper given at 36th Pugwash Symposium, London, 10-12 December).

57 *Hansard*, House of Commons, 6 April 1965, Col. 280.

58 President Kennedy, in *Washington Post*, 25 December 1962.

59 US Department of Defense Press Release, 28 July 1965.

60 Pym, F., 1981, The nuclear element for British defence policy, *R.U.S.I. Journal*, 126(2), 3-7.

61 Tornado. Watch it soar, *The Economist*, 21 February 1981.

62 Zuckerman, S., 1966, *Scientists and War*, London: Hamish Hamilton, Chapters 1-4.

63 *Hansard*, House of Commons, 14 December 1964, Col. 39.

64 Spinney, F.C., 1980, *Defense Facts of Life*, Office of the Assistant Secretary of Defense (Public Affairs).

65 *Hansard*, House of Commons, 16 December 1964, Col. 419.

66 *Hansard*, House of Commons, 19 May 1981, Col. 160.

67 Fallows, James, 1981, *National Defense*, Random House.

68 Fallows, James, 1981, The great defense deception, *New York Review of Books* (28 May).

69 Garwin, R.L., 1980, Bureaucratic and other problems in planning and managing military R & D, in Long & Reppy, *The Genesis of New Weapons*, London: Pergamon.

70 Clark, R.W., 1962, *The Rise of the Boffins*, London: Phoenix.

71 *Sunday Times*, 10 February 1980.

72 Owen, D., 1972, *The Politics of Defence*, London: Cape.

73 Owen, D., 1981, Submerge the Navy and sink the Trident, *Guardian* (1 June).

74 *Sunday Times*, 10 August 1980; and *Guardian*, 6 March 1981.

75 A summary of Tizard's paper to the Chiefs of Staff Committee is contained in Gowing, Margaret, 1974, *Independence and Deterrence*, London: Macmillan.

76 Blackett, P.M.S., 1948, *Military and Political Consequences of Atomic Energy*, London: Turnstile Press.

77 Goldschmidt, B., 1967, *Les Rivalités Atomiques, 1939–1966*, Paris: Fayard.

78 *SIPRI Yearbook of World Armaments and Disarmament* 1968/69, London: Duckworth, pp. 300 & 302.

79 Killian, J.R., 1977, *Sputniks, Scientists and Eisenhower*, Cambridge, Mass: MIT Press.

80 Kistiakowsky, G.B., 1967, *A Scientist at the White House*, Harvard: Harvard University Press.
    Kistiakowsky, G.B., 1979, False alarm: The story behind SALT II, *New York Review* (22 March).

81 Wiesner, J.B., 1965, *Where Science and Politics Meet*, New York: McGraw-Hill.

82 York, H., and G.A. Greb, 1979, *The Comprehensive Nuclear Test Ban* (Discussion Paper No. 84 at California Seminar on Arms Control and Foreign Policy, Santa Monica).

83 Jacobson, H.K., and E. Stein, 1966, *Diplomats, Scientists, and Politicians*, Ann Arbor: University of Michigan Press, p.462.

84 Hornig, D.F., 1980, in *Science Advice to the President*, ed. W. Golden, London: Pergamon.

85 Brennan, D.G., 1976, A comprehensive test ban: Everybody or nobody, *International Security*, 1(1), 92-117.

86 *Congressional Record* (HASC No.95-89), 13 October 1978.

87 Thurow, L., 1981, How to wreck the economy, *New York Review of Books*, (14 May).

88 Kaysen, C., 1968, Keeping the strategic balance, *Foreign Affairs*, 46(4), 665-675.

89 Ruina, J., 1981, *ABM Technology and Arms Control* (Paper presented at IFRI Colloq. Science and Disarmament, Paris, January).

90 Owen, D., 1981, *Face the Future*, London: Cape.

91 Foot, M., 1973, *Aneurin Bevan, 1945–1960*, London: Davis-Poynter.

92 Bolef, D.I., and M. Antell, 1968, Tactical nuclear weapons, *Scientist and Citizen* (reprinted in *Nuclear Weapons*, Department of Atomic Energy, Bombay, India, 1970.).

GLOSSARY

ABM an anti-ballistic missile (defence)

ACSP Advisory Council on Scientific Policy

ARPA Advanced Research Projects Agency

CEP circular error probable. Missiles and bombs rarely hit the precise spot at which they are aimed. By CEP is meant the radius of a circle whose centre is the aiming point, and within which 50 per cent of strikes should fall

Chevaline the code-name for a modification of the Polaris ballistic missile warhead designed to counter ABM defences, notably by incorporation of decoys

CND Campaign for Nuclear Disarmament

Counterforce US strategy in which military installations, eg missile silos, are the primary targets in retaliation against nuclear attack.

Countervalue US strategy in which cities and other civilian complexes are the principal targets in retaliation against nuclear attack.

Cruise a low-flying pilotless aircraft with either a conventional or a nuclear warhead (medium or long-range)

CTB Comprehensive Test-Ban Treaty

DRPC Defence Research Policy Committee

ER enhanced radiation (weapon), ie neutron bomb

ICBM an inter-continental ballistic missile

ICTB Inclusive Comprehensive Test-Ban Treaty

IRBM an intermediate-range ballistic missile

MAD mutually assured destruction

Manoeuvrable bus the section of a ballistic missile which carries the warheads, and whose speed and orientation is adjustable to allow each warhead to be directed independently onto its target

Minuteman a US land-based inter-continental ballistic missile

MIRV multiple independently targetable re-entry vehicles fitted to ballistic missiles

MX the code-name for a projected US mobile inter-continental ballistic missile

NATO North Atlantic Treaty Organisation

NPT Non-Proliferation Treaty

PD 59 Presidential Directive 59 (of 1980, defining US 'counterforce' strategy)

Pershing II a US medium-range ('theatre') ballistic missile

Polaris a submarine-launched intermediate/long-range ballistic missile

R and D research and development

SACEUR Supreme Allied Commander (Europe)

SALT Strategic Arms Limitation Talks/Treaty

SHAPE Supreme Headquarters Allied Powers Europe

Skybolt a US air-launched intermediate-range ballistic missile, whose development was stopped

SNDV strategic nuclear delivery vehicle

SS20 a Soviet mobile intermediate-range ballistic missile

throw-weight the total weight of the last stage carried by a ballistic missile

Trident a submarine-launched long-range ballistic missile

INDEX

About the Author

Solly Zuckerman began researching the biological effects of bomb blast for the British government at the start of World War II. After the war, he served on numerous councils and committees and was deputy chairman of the advisory council on scientific policy. From 1960 to 1966 he was chief scientific advisor to the Ministry of Defense and from 1966 to 1971 he was chief scientific advisor to the British Government. When he retired he was given a lifetime peerage. He is the author of numerous scientific works and of *Scientists and War* and *Beyond the Ivory Tower*. He lives in England.